D1243313

THE
UNPAINTED

Roger Ackling
Douglas Cocker
Thomas Joshua Cooper
Chris Drury
Ian Hamilton Finlay
Hamish Fulton
Andy Goldsworthy
Bernard Lassus
Richard Long
Raymond Moore
David Nash
Iain Patterson
Linda Taylor
David Tremlett
Herman de Vries

LANDSCAPE

Essays & Texts by
Simon Cutts
David Reason
Jonathan Williams
Lucius Burckhardt
Graeme Murray
John Bevis
Thomas A. Clark

1987

Coracle Press
Scottish Arts Council
Graeme Murray Gallery

The publishers gratefully acknowledge the financial assistance of the Trustees of the Henry Moore
Foundation.

ISBN 1 85119 014 7
Copyright © 1987
Coracle Press, London; Graeme Murray Gallery, Edinburgh; Scottish Arts Council, Edinburgh.

Designed at Coracle Press, London
Printed by Penshurst Press, Kent

Acknowledgements

To each artist: Roger Ackling, Douglas Cocker, Thomas Joshua Cooper, Chris Drury, Ian Hamilton Finlay, Hamish Fulton, Andy Goldsworthy, Bernard Lassus, Richard Long, Raymond Moore, David Nash, Iain Patterson, Linda Taylor, David Tremlett and Herman de Vries for the work and time spent on the demands of this exhibition and book. Each of these fifteen artists were invited to make new works for the exhibition as a result of their visiting Scotland. The Scottish Arts Council would like to thank the selectors of the exhibition, Simon Cutts and Graeme Murray, for their professional commitment and the enthusiasm they have shown for this project. To John Bevis, Lucius Burckhardt, Thomas A. Clark, David Reason and Jonathan Williams for their distinguished contributions to this book, and to Suzanne Marston for her Swiss-English to English translation of Lucius Burckhardt's essay; Ian Mackenzie and the School of Scottish Studies, Edinburgh, for allowing permission to reproduce the photographs in the section *Transients*; to Babs Sigurjonsson at the British Embassy in Reykjavik for her assistance in preparing the *Shorter Icelandic to English Dictionary*; James Hunter Blair for allowing David Nash to make a new work on the Blairquhan Estate in Ayrshire; to the proprietors of the Ben Alder Estate for permission to photograph Chris Drury's sculpture, and to the photographer Sean Hudson; and to the staff of the Royal Botanic Gardens, Edinburgh, for their guidance to Herman de Vries in planning his itinerary to the West coast of Scotland.

Photographic credits:

Derek Bayes: 19, 20; Robert Botsford: 112; Annemarie Burckhardt: 106-108; Lucius Burckhardt: 111; Thomas Joshua Cooper: 66-67; Prudence Cummings Associates: 17; Andy Dewar: 41; Michael Duffett: 18, 23, 61, 77-79; Hamish Fulton: 15, 85; Andy Goldsworthy: 53-55; Hamish Henderson: 113; Sean Hudson: 69, 72, 73; Helge Johnnysen: 16; Richard Kearton: 129, 131, 133; Werner Kissling: 118; Bernard Lassus: 37-39; Roger Leitch: 116, 117; Richard Long: 22; Ian Mackenzie: 114; Raymond Moore: 43-45; David Nash: 47; Monika Nikolic: 96, 101, 105; Iain Patterson: 49-51; Antonia Reeve: 59; Gail Ridgewell: 21; S.F. Sanderson: 115; Bruno Schneyer: 8; David Tremlett: 57; Herman de Vries: 61; G.K. Yates: 135.

Foreword

When James Bustard of the Scottish Arts Council asked Coracle for an exhibition of very physical, literalistic sculpture, in the wake of our *Tongue & Groove* exhibition, it was already too late. It was the very early spring of 1984, and the mind had begun to drift back to some of the continuing themes, of landscape, of a non-mimetic art of time and placement, resulting from the particularisation of minimal and conceptual art in our own context.

The first notion for an exhibition was prepared, with some fifteen artists. The focus of Scotland as the base for an exhibition was an intact idea with no element of spurious appeasement, and it was obvious that we should invite our friend Graeme Murray, the most persistent gallerist of sensibility, to develop the Scottish centrality of the exhibition. At the same time he would bring newer and younger elements into the final assembly.

Writers were invited to expand the context of the exhibition and to look towards Europe, and at the same time to deal with the specific works created for a commissioning exhibition.

In the summer of 1984 I laboured with a spade about my house and garden in Norfolk and on the title for the exhibition. That which emerged still gives me much pleasure.

This book, as ever for Coracle, is pivotal to the exhibition. We fought for its format and arrangement amongst ourselves. It is a start, a way of seeing the advancement that some of these artists have made over the last twenty years.

Simon Cutts
Coracle
November 1986

herman de vries in his 200km² atelier

Notes on The Unpainted Landscape

Simon Cutts

'Take up your Brushes, gentlemen.
It is six o'clock, and chrome-yellow
has come into the landscape.'
– *a painter of Barbizon*

When we think of the landscape and of an art derived from it, we may bring to mind first of all the activity of drawing and painting. The image is redolent, of a solitary wind-blown figure in front of an easel. It is almost as inherent a cliché as the garret or attic for the isolate artist in an urban parallel. With the selection presented here, we hope to show the work of some artists who, whilst working with the landscape, do so in another way. They do not try to reproduce the appearance of the landscape by way of painted effects. The intrinsic correspondence between the devices of painting and the imposing scene in front of us has been central to our experience of art, as in the tradition and effects of watercolour.

Nonetheless, in the period of the last twenty years, some artists have established new procedures for an art of landscape, and have chosen to work with wider means at their disposal. They have used the recording photograph, the idea of time and sequence to make a journey, the notion of change and substitution in a place. In fact they have re-examined the composition of an art related to landscape.

It would be folly to dismember the fragrant ambiguity of the title, but at first it pre-supposes an unchartedness that for these islands could be taken as Scotland. It is not incidental that many of these artists have made work there previously, and it was of formative interest that many of the home-based artists had a relationship with Scotland. Its use as the site for our exhibition had a sense of scale and compactness that matched the intentions of our anthology.

Concurrent with a critical playfulness in the editing of this material, there is an ideological leaning. We wanted to suggest an underlying theoretical approach, a hardness of purpose, and with such intention we invited these writers and critics. Recent crops of exhibitions and essays have done very little to examine the procedural basis from which the work of many of these artists arises. Often they have failed to differentiate the approach of various artists, and have preferred instead the cultural tokenism of the presence of artists in general. The aspirations of the ecology movement may do almost nothing to lift this work from the coffee-table or to prevent its association with aspects of the leisure industry.

Nature is only an idea *said Delacroix*

David Tremlett opened up his tape-recorder on a journey in 1972 in each of the old counties: Murrayshire, Morayshire, Westmoreland, etc. The random sound of *The Spring recordings* becomes its own pastoral, of birdsong, of wind, of movement in the landscape. The work is presented as a shelf of eighty-one tapes, each one lasting for thirty minutes. It sits as a silent wall work, referring to its source and its potential replay.

It reminds me of the absence of particularised composition in the work of Hamish Fulton. A work is completely homogenous in character, and the photograph we, are presented with and its text are a moment's cross-section through a journey. Although he has made many splendid photographs in seemingly exotic places, Fulton's work gives me most delight when the photograph has an arbitrary quality, is less skillful, and provides a more silent crux for the relation of text and image. The line of birds in *Dirt Road Bird Song* almost follows the rhythm of the words of the text. In *Rain in the Manifold Valley,* this very quality of the indifference of the photograph is the perfect rest for the resonance of its sub-title 'Conversations of Other Walks'.

Of differing concentration, and much more classically contrived, are the photographs of Thomas Joshua Cooper. He lumbers his heavy equipment along crags and gulleys, hung from trees on ropes, in remote places. He continues the tradition of the landscape photographer. The redemption and singularity of Cooper's work, its burnished detail and internality, lifts it from the glib medium of photography to form its own genre.

Roger Ackling burns points and lines with a glass lens by focussing the radiations of the sun. He does this in the context of a formal work using a printed mount and a framed presentation, or else on loose individual objects found on particular journeys. These can be pieces of driftwood, even bone, or once in Japan rectangular piano hammers. Their place of origin is always a specific part of the context of a work, as is the time taken, and the furriness of the burned line. Spectacular possibilities for Ackling's work have been the series *Drawings from Behind Clouds,* where the intermittent line is the result of the sun disappearing behind and reappearing from the clouds. A highly precise and formal work was made by Roger Ackling in 1978 entitled *Five Sunsets in One Hour.* Here he walked up a hill on the Isle of Wight and burned with his glass for one minute at five intervals up the hill, using the final rays of the setting sun in each case. The higher he climbed, the weaker the rays of the sun became, and in consequence the shorter the burned lines.

I can understand the appeal of Andy Goldsworthy's leaf-box constructions, his grass-stalk line held in place by blackthorns, his arrangements of the various russets of autumn leaves, but I confess to a leaning for his more urban works. A large snowball made the previous winter and kept in a deep-freeze was brought into the gallery at Coracle in Camberwell in May 1985, and melted slowly over a period of some four days to leave only a debris of twigs and leaves from the place of its accumulation. In the same exhibition, but in another room, Andy Goldsworthy prepared one of his 'holes'. By cutting through the lino and the floorboards underneath, and the joists that could be seen from ground level, he created an unexplained void of the basement beneath, of such blackness and density to be purely optical; the hole could at times almost float in the room. By far the most spectacular of his holes was made in the Serpentine Gallery in the exhibition *Salon d'Automne* during October 1984, when Goldsworthy dug under the gallery a space of about his own cubic capacity. The gaping chasm was then patched with twigs and leaves, narrowing the orifice to a neat hole about four inches in diameter. The earth removed from underneath was carefully replaced on this membrane. In a circle of the remaining soil, another inexplicable blackness floated, almost like a patch of soot.

The work of Chris Drury appears to have developed out of the aesthetics and attitudes of landscape artists of a seemingly previous generation. His work incorporates very different source material and culture from his forerunners. He has also re-evaluated as a genuine influence on his work elements of craft, elements of folk-culture and the work of the artisan. At times his work attempts an ordinariness of purpose that almost defies art. The totemic work *'Medicine Wheel'* from 1982-83 is the ordering of an activity that many people partake of, the collecting and assembling of items from nature. Chris Drury arranged these objects, one found per day over the entire year, into a calendar of parts, which could be read from the accompanying lexical key. Almost the next work he made was its exact opposite in form. The *'Medicine Basket'* contains all the dried plants that in minute quantities act medicinally, but in larger doses are severe poisons. The theme of the basket as a woven or cast container, of an active or narrative development, continues to preoccupy Drury's work, made on journeys, or afterwards, involving the dreams affected by a place.

Ian Hamilton Finlay's great contribution to an art of landscape has been the development of his metaphoric garden 'Little Sparta' in the Pentland foothills at Dunsyre, Lanarkshire. Here over the last twenty years he has refined the generic forms that reflect his concerns as a poet. From the Concrete Poem of the mid-sixties, to the Epic of the Second World War and now through the Revolutionary period, Finlay has assembled his dictionary of cultural styles and emblems. Working in collaboration with other artists and craftsmen he has made the works which accompany the vistas and walks of Little Sparta. At the side of the gardens the Garden Temple serves as a gallery for installed works. It is Finlay's sense of poem and placement that exemplifies his concerns, the signs and sounds of words engrained in their objects.

The brevity of these notes prevents a detailed view of the multiplicity of strategies in the works of Richard Long. That is for another occasion. Richard Long has made work from the walk, from the marked map, from an arrangement made on a walk and presented photographically. He has made work in galleries from particular material observed on walks. He has made works with words in plain sequential listings and in more complex literal arrangements. He has made works with books, from an implicit understanding of their editioned nature. For all these he has often used very simple devices; the circle, the cross, the spiral, the straight line. Inside these forms he has relied on a matter-of-fact placement of the material that demonstrates his skill-less activity. There are no tricks, and the work can be remade at any time. *'Magpie Line'*, 1985 uses chalk flints as its material. Its black-and-whiteness carries and associates its title in a particularly English way. With such components he creates an order that is not dissimilar to his anticipation of the empathetic form of the organic world, the patterning of driftwood, the spiral rhythm of debris at a dam.

To those I have not mentioned and for those not included in this exhibition, notably Lothar Baumgarten, Nicklaus Lang and Wolfgang Laib, a continuing regard for their work.

14 **David Tremlett**
The Spring recordings, 1972 *detail*

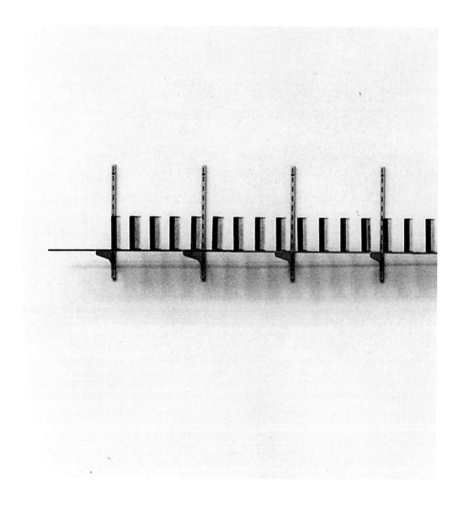

opposite: **Hamish Fulton** Dirt Road Bird Song, 1978

DIRT ROAD   BIRD SONG

A 115 MILE WALK ICELAND SPRING 1978

Andy Goldsworthy
Turf roll *and* Snowball, 1985

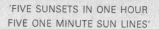

'FIVE SUNSETS IN ONE HOUR
FIVE ONE MINUTE SUN LINES'

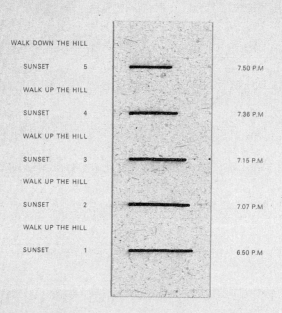

WALK DOWN THE HILL

SUNSET   5   7.50 P.M

WALK UP THE HILL

SUNSET   4   7.36 P.M

WALK UP THE HILL

SUNSET   3   7.15 P.M

WALK UP THE HILL

SUNSET   2   7.07 P.M

WALK UP THE HILL

SUNSET   1   6.50 P.M

A COUNTRY SKETCH
CHILLERTON DOWN ISLE OF WIGHT ENGLAND
JUNE 24 1978

Medicine Wheel, 1982-3
One natural object for each day of the year

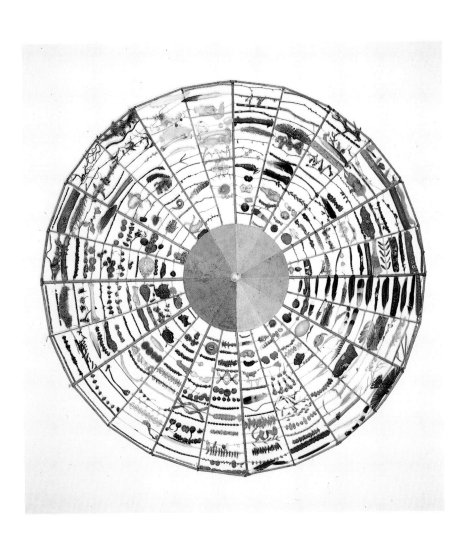

20 **Chris Drury**
Medicine Basket, 1984

Wood Angelica, Belladonna, Bindweed, Black Bryony, Bluebell, Box, Bracken, Broom, Burdock, Cotoneaster, Cowbane, Cowslip, Cuckoopint, Dock, Dropwort, Foxglove, Heather, Hellebore, Hemlock, Hemlock Water Dropwort, Henbane, Herb Robert, Hogweed, Holly, Iris, Ivy, Ladies Bedstraw, Laurel, Tree Lupin, Mignonette, Mistletoe, Mugwort, Field Mustard, Hedge Mustard, Woody Nightshade, Plantain, Poppy, Sea Poppy, Privet, Purging Flax, Ragwort, Sea Spurge, Sun Spurge, Sorrel, Spindle, St Johns Wort, Great Burnet Saxifrage, Tansy, Thorn Apple, Toadflax, Travellers Joy, Common Vetch, Vipers Bugloss, Wayfaring Tree, Yellow Rattle, Yew.

22 **Richard Long**
Magpie Line, 1985

rosa damascena

eschenau summer press, edition of 100, 1984

A Hard Singing of Country

David Reason

a slender horizon of words

The warrior Nobumitsu came to see Ekichu, the 7th master of Jukukuji and a famous painter. The visitor challenged Ekichu: quoting the famous Zen phrase 'A finger direct to the human heart, see the nature to be Buddha', Nobumitsu asked for a picture of the heart. The teacher picked up his brush and flicked a spot of ink into Nobumitsu's face. The warrior was surprised and annoyed, and Ekichu rapidly sketched the angry face.

Then Nobumitsu asked for a picture of the 'nature' as in the phrase 'see the nature'. Ekichu broke the brush and said: 'That's the picture'.

Art is dumb. The work of art is, unlike nature, incomplete. Being a work it is informed by deliberation and choice, however spontaneous and unreflective the artistic process may appear to be: just to acknowledge the autonomy of the work is to assume sufficient responsibility for bringing it into the world. Thus the work embodies an attitude towards that world, and willy nilly it is a cognitively and ethically saturated object – judgements seem inescapable. Being incomplete, a fragment broken off from its history, an intruder, the way things are a stranger never quite at ease, at home, the work of art also presents an enigma, a riddle. Solving a riddle in art is to indentify the reason why it is insoluble, to clarify the nature of the displacement of registration between the art and the world. (In that authentic art invokes a utopian perspective, we should find such parallax both unsurprising and profoundly disturbing).

The work of art is not self-sufficient, and being speechless it inevitably tempts word and thought. The work of art is *completed* in intepretation, commentary and criticism, not in the sense of being finished (off), but as an electrical circuit may be completed, a switch closed – so that energy may flow, so that the power of the assembly may be realised. Art seems inevitably to be taken up in discourse. We require knowledge of some relevant artistic or cultural tradition before being able to employ the appropriate conventions for appreciation of a work, and a tradition is intimately bound up with canons of criticism. Moreover, artistic production always addresses an audience, even if antagonistically, (and secretly), and thus calls on an interlocutor whose achievement is to call out the speech that lies in the work. In these ways, the work of art is given voice.

But art is not a substitute for speech. Art can say what we cannot say. Whilst an intelligent response to authentic art may lead us to become articulate where before we were dumb (expanding our (self-) understanding, and vouchsafing a warrant for the utopian perspective), we are also assured that art can – indeed, must – go beyond speech. Artworks are not so much anticipatory in their content – prefiguring the good life to come – as ecstatic, securing the conviction that things might really be otherwise than they are. We need to go through a speaking of art in order to confirm that the wisdom of art is in its – and our – practice. Authentic art shows us ways in which we may go on, taking up not only the field of possibilities which it maps out but the talisman of *maybe* itself (the work of art a dowsing rod, indicating buried freedoms). And in compelling us to reassess the tradition to which it relates, authentic art loosens the hold that history has on our collar.

Ethical considerations are embodied in artistic practice. Art is dumb because, since speaking is never decisive in compelling our assent to the good life, it must strive to transcend speech. Having spoken, we must attend to the presence of the work and the practice in their particularity, not as a remainder or excess left over from our discussions, but as the axis of its being a work of art.

Landscape – the art world's code word for nature – has become an awkward term for us, and this is a measure of the force of the ethical imperatives which are inescapable in considering landscape art today. In a fashion that strikingly parallels the controversial character of the nude in contemporary visual art, art which implicates and invokes the aesthetics of landscape is committed to participating in the politics of nature and the environment. Western societies no longer sustain even the pretence of a consensus over the proper utilization of the earth's resources, and so conceptions of nature and of landscape mark out the ground for political debate.

Correspondingly, the idea of 'landscape' implies a particular conception of nature and what we may do with the natural world. Generally, nature tends to be seen in one of three ways: as the antithesis of culture; as defined by humanity's interest in dominating the world; and as culture itself. The first of these views stresses a radical difference between nature and everything human: nature is precisely that which is neither human nor of human origin, and key terms, which both describe and evaluate the natural world, are 'wild', 'wilderness', 'remote' and 'unspoilt'. The second perspective recognises both that human beings are interacting with the natural world, and that the latter is thereby changed; but that world is still considered as alien to us (and, insofar as human beings are a part of nature, we are rendered alien to ourselves) for we apprehend nature only as a realm to be moulded, manipulated and exploited by us. In the context of landscape art, we find this domain inhabited by large-scale earth works, a concern with the domesticated environment of agricultural regions, and the celebration of gardens. (Since we are here dealing with the social organisations of the natural world, it is inevitable that the social arrangements of people are implicated in these arenas of interest. Earth moving is associated with areas of low land-value, marginal land often occupied by marginalised peoples; and both agriculture and the construction and maintenance of a discourse of gardens has involved the subordination of a workforce). Lastly, the identification of nature with culture reflects the historical development of humanity's relationship with a natural world which can only be known through that changing relationship. However, it also elaborates the temptation to see nature after our image, and not only to oppose necessity and freedom, rationality and non-rationality (spontaneity, determinism, irrationality), but to narcissistically identify them with a fiction conjured beyond the factory gate and domestic latch.

In each case, nature is revealed only in relation to something else, as one member of a couple. And in the light of the multivalences displayed I have two remarks I wish to stress. First, that history, as what has passed, is presented to us as an apparent nature; similarly, nature itself must be seen as transitory, passing, and therefore intrinsically historical. In this sense, all history is the history of the fall of nature: Thoreau's anguished cry – 'Is it not a maimed and imperfect naure that I am conversant with?' – is always true and always misleading.

And so to my second point: namely, that all nature is second nature. All nature has been produced, worked and influenced, primarily by man, but also, of course, by the community of plants and animals (and associated physical processes). For example, the massive deforestation of Scotland has resulted from interventions that date back at least 1000 years. Trees were felled for economic reasons (to clear land for fields, to procure building timbers, to produce wood for charcoal burning) and to enhance security (destroying the habitat of wolves, or the refuges of outlaws and bandits). In recent years, the rapid decrease in the size of upland woodlands is largely due to the mismanagement of inappropriate exploitation, for example, overgrazing and moor-burning. However, although all landscapes are the expression of past economy (or: are habitats for ghosts), not all economies are oriented to the same ends. Whereas contemporary practices typically aim to secure a commercial profit, many other peoples (famously some – but not all – American Indians) have shaped their environments so as to secure a greater security of livelihood, commonly through a planned diversification of production and resource use.

Of course, not all environments have suffered as has Scotland the effects of 'The Coming of the Sheep' and the Clearances following Culloden, events which ensure that the bare hills are like cairns of lament and indictment. However, no society is stable, and the environmental consequences of human occupancy extend far beyond mere political boundaries. The one sure lesson of history is that there is history: flux and change are in the nature of things. Engels, reflecting on the philosophy of Feuerbach, considered that 'the world is not to be comprehended as a complex of ready-made *things,* but as a complex of *processes,* in which the things apparently stable no less than their mind images in our heads, the concepts, go through an uninterrupted change of coming into being and passing away...'. The visions and theories of nature which we and other peoples form are as transient as nature itself. The versions of natural relationship we may sometimes cherish as intimating a more harmonious and integral bond between humanity and the natural world than we enjoy – amounting, indeed, for us, to an assurance of the possibility of a lived reconciliation with nature, and often instanced by the cosmologies of the Plains Indians of nineteenth-century America and the Australian Aborigines of early twentieth-century Australia – these reflections, principles and protocols must be seen as the product of changing circumstances.

Neither ignorance nor beliefs shot through with convictions of 'sacredness' can guarantee to sustain the natural environment. The idea that direct productive involvement with the land, unmediated by the market, results in being in some obscure sense 'close to nature', and the hope that such apparent immediacy is equivalent to being in a better position to *know* nature, are products of misguided desire on our part. The practical attitude has ever been a prime source of mystification and error, and there is little in human history to nourish the thought that *living* through day-to-day concerns implies *seeing* through those day-to-day concerns. W.C. Fields reminded us that the perception of nature is dependent upon our viewpoint when explaining his aversion to drinking water: 'Fish fuck in it'. For anyone who seeks reassurance on the acuity of the natural or practical attitude, the common lore of rural Britain in the eighteenth and nineteenth centuries unearthed by Keith Thomas makes a sorry catalogue: to beget male lambs, the wind must be in the north; elm trees would grow from old chips and shavings; the hare changed its sex and slept with one eye open; the osprey was commonly believed to have one webbed foot (for swimming) and one clawed foot (for catching its prey). Nobody in the eighteenth century believed that swallows migrated to another country; the theory was that they dived into ponds and hibernated in the mud. Clearly, the knowledge of nature that we would seek is not just reverential, emphasising a need to show respect for nature, but also aspires to accuracy. Such understanding is only to be acquired by a scrupulous attention to things as they are, which is not so much a demand for right thinking as for right practice.

The pre-modern era in Western Europe cleaved to conceptions of the world which stressed, in mystified amd mystical form, the interdependence of human beings and the natural world. Christian and non-Christian alike found in natural events and phenomena the characteristics of a legible script: the world was a text which expressed intention, morality and significance. The development of industrial capitalism was accompanied by the leaching of wonder, and the percolation of disenchantment. The new world, recognisably modern, recognisably our own, accented the rationalisation not only of industrial production but also of everyday life. A new spirit of calculation replaced the older moral economy, and mystery gave way not so much to intelligibility as to the belief that things were intelligible in principle. Social relations of moral dependency became subject to a new morality of managerialism, and concurrently politics separated from everyday life and became subject to the overriding claims of expediency. With this cosmological disintegration arose the production of a disjunction between the inner and the outer life: people, radically alienated, now as then find little solace in the construction of a private sphere, socially and mentally. (Intriguingly, Freud's *Introductory Lectures on Psycholanalysis* contains this suggestive passage: 'The creation of the mental realm of phantasy finds a perfect parallel in the establishment of 'reservations' or 'nature reserves' in places where the requirements of agriculture, communications and industry threaten to bring about changes in the original face of the earth which will quickly make it unrecognisable. A nature reserve preserves its original state which everywhere else has to our regret been sacrificed to necessity. Everything, including what is useless and even what is noxious, can grow and proliferate there as it pleases.' Perhaps we should consider National Parks as accommodations to our despair.)

The past twenty years have seen the emergence of a more general and articulate interest in recovering something of the sense of the world and of our place in it. Habermas construes this as a historically significant shift of the leading edge of social concern from problems of distribution to the grammar of forms of life. Concomitantly, there is an evident attempt to 're-enchant' the world. This has both regressive and progressive aspects. Regressively, it involves the uncritical appropriation and colonization of historical moments and ideologies and exotic systems of belief. It is not merely silly, but also an example of the most unabashed arrogance, to pretend to be a Siberian shaman in Edinburgh or a Leveller in Luton. In any case, history has already ensured that such attempts to recapture the centre stage are doomed to marginalisation. ('Hegel somewhere remarks that all facts and personages of great importance in world history occur, as it were, twice. He forgot to add: the first time as tragedy, the second as farce'. So far as I know, Hegel said no such thing: however, Marx's generosity here is matched by his own oversight: for at the third and subsequent appearances, we are given pure soap-opera). Credulously embracing the occult, superstition and historical tableaux is absurd, but these resources have nonetheless provided characteristically critical bases from which to prise open the cracks of possibility in contemporary consciousness. It is through the imaginative re-awakening of the present that the glow of re-enchantment is produced. In the context of art, this promotes a practice which seeks to open up new possibilities in a way which is generally accessible, an art in which the inexhaustible particularity of the work is both testimony and promise of significance. In this context, an artistic practice which demands erudition and exegesis runs the risk of colluding in a cognitive and social closure: its esoteric appreciation not only panders to a sense of belonging to the right club, but the completion of the jigsaw produces little more than the satisfactions of arithmetic well done. (This is a thorny area, for insofar as esoteric knowledge is knowledge of a forgotten, ignored or suppressed tradition or history which is nonetheless productive of the current situation, then to intrigue the spectator into discovering that background which is necessary to understanding the work of art is, at the same time, to restore a constitutive element of identity which places the spectator in a better position to go on, now knowing where she/he stands). In all events the progressive aspects of 'other cultures' is apparent only with dedication to the search for a more exact knowledge of self and the social and natural environment.

'Here one's life and experience are so intense; one doesn't just belong, one is part of the landscape. The unhurried pace is easily accepted. In Europe I couldn't wait to see you again. I was so impatient and edgy. But in Nepal as each day passed I became more relaxed. I just kept going and going, looking at everything and drinking it all in. I have talked with the people and drunk tea in their houses. In Tengpoche we stayed an extra day simply because it was so beautiful. It was suddenly not so important whether I met you today or tomorrow, and so perhaps my joy in finding you is more than those heady days in Europe.'
Uschi Messner

I am disturbed by the fascination which the photograph exercises over me. To some extent, I suspect that this is because the image is, really, caused by or, better, intimately connected with its subject (or is it object?): the photograph is both image and (an extention of) the thing itself. We seem to *possess* that which the photograph pictures: or, with slightly less supernatural aura, we *access* the real through the mediation of causality. (Samuel Morse remarked of Daguerrotypes that 'they cannot be called copies of nature, but portions of nature herself.') Moreover, the vivid fullness and density of the image, perhaps most noticeable in the cumbersome precursors to modern photography, produces an almost hallucinatory sense of verisimilitude. Take a lens, and on a bright day project the scene onto the palm of your hand: here is a world of toys, miniatures, mannequins, Lilliputians. The intensities of this reduced enactment of the world, this condensation of the magic of reality being as it is, is itself magic. Smallness is important: the advertising hoarding seems to potlatch its semiotic wealth, it is profligate and extravagant with its signs. Where the billboard shouts, the small

Leaf of a Plant, 1844
plate 7 from *The Pencil of Nature*

mannequins in my hand are mute in focussed silence.

In the camera obscura at Bristol, the panorama is projected onto a shallow concave table in the centre of the room. The road leads past the houses towards the bridge. See that figure on the bridge? He or she (does it matter which?) jumps off the parapet: I imagine my hand plunging into the image, a saving gesture. For a moment, the suicide is cradled in my palm.

The analysis of photographic fascination requires a concept of witnessing that involves the world reaching out to us, coming through the imaginary surface of the image. In an important sense, the witness lets the scene in, a hospitality whose epistemological standing is resolved in the necessity for us to have survived as a species. Were I placed beyond the dubious safety net of hi-tech, I would have to learn to remove my conceptual blinds and let the light of the world in. However, the position of witness is not passive, for it must be grounded in an active perception, the movement of conscious being in the world. The world is there to be embraced, accepted, lived in.

The photograph stands in the place of a witness of a world immobile. This stilling of the flow of life resembles the achievement of a tableau in Victorian theatre: within the frame, a point is made, summation given, an attitude struck – the image seems stuffed with significance. The photograph creates the occasion: a momentary pause, a caesura, for contemplation and reflection. (The photograph sometimes seems like a moment in the children's game 'Statues': the music is just out of earshot, in the future still, and we are left with a gesture of tense clarity of trembling exactness). Or conversely (and this amounts to the same thing) the photograph is perceived as governed by a fermata, creating the effect of an extreme dilation of time. In the photographic image, nothing is changed except the imminence of fulfilment: the catastrophe is postponed. So in representing reality, the photograph puts 'it' in quotation marks. Is this why the image seems to stand off from particularity, generalising the scene it purports to depict? Is this the condition which allows them to 'accumulate historicity' (as Stephen Bann puts it) – the quotation marks the walls of a vessel, the photograph a basin of time?

Reflecting on the nude in art, Adrian Stokes writes 'as we have noted in the use to which actuality is put by the art of collage, actuality, and therefore the gaze of science, isolates and illicits phantasy as a stupendous force. A part of the aesthetic stress upon the actual is stress upon the corporeal content in phantasy.'

The photograph, if not actually a slice of reality, seems to be the next best thing: a direct impression of the existent world – and we would take embossing, watermarks, and the traces, signs and tracks of natural processes and beings to be similar in this respect. Actuality can be indisputably brought within my reach, but the index of reality furnished by the camera serves as witness to what was there, before the lens, only insofar as I have an appropriate, accurate understanding of the processes of image formation. And even then, knowing that this image is caused by a portion of the real world, I do not know what it is a photograph *of* unless I know something of how that world comes to be as it is, for identity is always a matter of catching up with history. As Brecht pointed out, the photograph of Krupps' factory may not show the actuality directly, in that that is grounded in a reticulation of social relations; but to the extent that I am sure that there is an actuality there, then I am also confident that I already know something of the social relations in which it is embedded. The photograph's fascination is a fascination at finding what I had forgotten I had put there, its magic is the magic of recalling what we always already knew.

Do I dwell in my body? Then my body and its flesh, this house and the land become metaphors of and for each other. Remove the house – and with it the sense of landscape that encompasses everything from the window-sill to the final spectacle before the horizon – and I am thrown open to the land and move inevitably towards my horizon. My world ends at the horizon, the beyond which we will never see: I imagine the world a century, generations hence – how can that be my world, our world, when knowledge of its becoming so decisively eludes our grasp. At my death, I provide the stuff of the earth. The Mesolithic cist grave (stone chamber with a stone slab roof) contains a body (it must have been fresh packed) curled into a position which many archaeologists scrupulously avoid calling *foetal*: in death, at the origin of an inner horizon beyond which we cannot see or go, we prepare for rebirth. It is possible that this return to a foetal position is simply a way of marking an end, just as some symphonies are finished off with the return of their opening bars. It is also possible that this gesture towards a myth of eternal returns wards off the identification of these horizons of life and land with language, that horizon beyond which we fear to go else we lose meaning. Whatever the feints and decoys, be assured we join the earth when we meet our horizon at the centre of the circling world.

Our graves are marked with a stone, an effigy, or a simple plaque. The traces of a worked land function that way also: a hillside's ancient terraces of cultivation shadowed in the glancing sun, the deforested moor, the wholesale transformation of nature that human beings wantonly and often unwittingly bring about – are grave markers to our ancestors and ourselves.

For some artists simply getting to grips with the world in walking, camping or sitting, having a direct relationship with that nature which is to be celebrated in their art, provides the means by which to get behind the conceptual blinkers of a mundane life and experience the landscape as what it is. Their presence in nature is a palpable absence in the work which is everywhere implied in the work itself. The presence of the body is indirect, an elusive presence which is palpably and tangibly there. It is the presence of the body implied by the hand through the grating, a faint cry of help, a scrawled message on the back of a post card. If western art is indeed to be characterised as revolving around the impossibility of representing the body in its presence as Schefer argues, then those artists who turn their back on their ego pay no attention to it. They allow for the body in the landscape.

The life-cycle of creation is endless. We watch the seasons come and go, life into life forever. The child becomes parent, who then becomes respected elder. Life, so sacred; it is good to be a part of it all.
Anonymous American Indian

A Hard Singing of Country

rediscovering silence

William Gilpin's experience of Scotland in the late eighteenth century led him to oppose Dr. Johnson's judgement that it provided the civilised eye with a 'wide extent of hopeless sterility'. He rejected Johnson's anthropocentric conception of 'uselessness' in favour of a consideration of 'use in nature' as a measure of wealth. However, it is not certain that with this criterion Gilpin was anticipating an ecological philosophy, for his notion of 'use' relates primarily to a context of the aesthetics of the picturesque:

'A mountain is of use sometimes to close a distance by an elegant, varied line; and sometimes to come in as a second ground, hanging over a lake, or forming a screen to the nearer objects. To each purpose the Scottish mountains are well adapted...'

Following Gilpin's footsteps nowadays is not to be caught seeking the picturesque in Scotland, but involves, perhaps, travelling to Alaska, a place that as the surrealists realised occupies a similar position in the current cartography of desire.

Bernard Lassus made a trip to Alaska in the summer of 1985. Modern travel – the flight out and back, cruising on the *Rhapsody* – provides distinctive vantage points from which to take in the view, and a camera records the passing scene with more ease than had the artist been reliant on a sketchbook. A series of reflections suggest themselves, circulating around the axis of a history that has constituted the possibility of comparison, such as a collection of postcards might revolve on a newsagent's carousel: the differences in transport then and now, and how this might affect the traveller's experience of place; the consequences of the absorption of conventions of the picturesque into popular consciousness for seeing the landscape; the effects of changes in the technology of representation on the theory of representation; the relationship of their respective notions of the exotic. All interesting issues. But I am hooked by three things; the thought that the photograph (and especially these tourist snaps) witnesses what is actually there; the commonplace that we travel to find an image of ourselves; and the observation that what is here represented are, precisely, the *conditions* of travel (the factors that enable some particular perspective to be taken) not the object photographed, which as the projected subject forever eludes the function of actuality. Consequently my gaze lingers over a shot from the deck of the *Rhapsody* showing the quayside, the rock face behind. Each boat operating from this location seems to have left its marque, at least since 1961. Names, alphabets, advertisements jostle for a niche, for some purchase: from 'ΣAM' to '41 DAYS OUT', the rock is cluttered with a passing human presence, which insists that the altered stone be its witness. And Soapy Smith pictured the skull in the landscape, staring empty-eyed away from such flamboyant significance in a gesture unnoticed by *The Skagway News*.

Bernard Lassus
pp 37-39: *from* Voyages en Alaska, été, 1985
Hommage à William Gilpin

There is a circle of the touched and the touching, the touched takes hold of the touching; there is a circle of the visible and the seeing, the seeing is not without visible existence; there is even an inscription of the touching in the visible, of the seeing in the tangible – and the converse...

Merleau-Ponty

Landscapes change; and change is itself an intrinsic aspect of our experience of landscape. The landscape is a polyrhythmic composition of processes whose pulse varies from the erratic flutter of leaves to the measured drift and clash of tectonic plates. Relative to the human span, the view before us seems composed of fleeting, ephemeral effects which create a patina of transience on apparently stable forms. Douglas Cocker's sculptures *Silver Kiss/Rough Touch* stress the temporal quality of landscape through their play on similarity and difference – their palpable difference of texture proclaims their clear similarity of form. Here, in work inspired by seeing the hill known as Craigendarroch under varying conditions of climate and season, Cocker lets the texture of light rub against the grain of landscape. Each of these wayward doubles has a cloud as familiar: in one, it seems to float, barely tethered to the summit, tingling to drift away, whilst the other seems oppressively cloud-laden. The relationship between hill and cloud and between hill and hill resounds with a harmony that the artist finds it impossible to discern in contemporary society. Nature is therefore pressed into service to indict society.

Silver Kiss / Rough Touch, 1986

In the mist signs proliferate. A young tree beside a truncated stump (matricide?) (we are on the verge of Oedipal readings here), one arm of a signpost and what seems to be an inn sign blank beneath its legend. The grey substantial light comes between objects, isolating them: the junction becomes a collection of enigmatic ciphers, the mist has created a collage.

Raymond Moore's careful photographs show the margins and transitional spaces of a human world. If it is true that the texture of civilisation is now that of marginality, then Moore is an artist who stumbles upon unoccupied zones on our doorstep. He photographs a world seen on edge, where all boundaries are thresholds. His control of tone, texture and composition (and often his fascination with reflections) emphasises the camera's lack of any sense of distance or depth: paradoxically, the viewer's eye teeters on the tip of a vertiginous space. These pictures generate a sense of a detailed otherness lingering beneath an ordinarily known world; as if we were noticing a face in sleep. This aura of alterity resonates with the ecstatic aura of premonition that some epileptics report as preceding a fit.

Slightly scary though it is (I too hold my breath), Moore's photographic attention to this nonetheless unaccustomed otherness attests to a perception and a possibility of living life differently. Yet it simultaneously reconciles us to the world as it is by rendering it as a cornucopia (:cornutopia?) of wayward pleasures. Postponing our date with liberation, we pick over the junkyard of historical contingency. These photographs are disturbing because they insist upon the doubts we would rather lose in the mist of everyday concerns. We seek to haunt these scenes as ghosts.

Dumfriesshire, 1985

44 **Raymond Moore**
Gigha, 1985

Kintyre, 1985

From a fallen oak David Nash hews a boat shaped like a double wishbone. This shape is immanent in the tree, its possibility characteristic of what the tree is. Nash conceives of a world woven of primitive elements (space, earth, air, water and fire) and his art as a way of attending to the way things are in the world. His is a domain of neither wilderness nor town, rather he stresses the axial nature of our productive involvement with the land. In agricultural practices throughout the world, trees have comprised both a resource (for building and burning) and a limit (to the size of crop fields), and have been both treated as vegetable vermin and revered. Nash considers wood the pre-eminent material for engaging the elements, poetically and practically. He extends farming techniques to his artistic ends, and fire is the most protean of these tools. Fire solders microchips and produces continental grasslands. The *Elemental Boat* focusses these elements in a three-hour ritual of cauterisation and quenching, annealing the surface of the cut wood and charring it to a parody of bark. Nash's is a disturbing art, for its use of land-management techniques in the absence of an economic necessity can highlight that myopic reconstruction of the natural world that is indeed the aim and consequence of an agriculture that seeks to dominate nature with its unnaturing practices.

Elemental Boat; River Girvan, Ayrshire, 1986

Rearrange your stag heads: here are 100 trophies of peak experience. What was once an ecstatic experience, proper to the awesome character of mountains, becomes for some climbers merely another victory over natural adversity. The goal of climbing every mountain transforms quality into quantity, and for the Munro who has everything under his belt, Iain Patterson offers one hundred brand new summits to scale. These porcelain miniatures held abrasively arrayed on the wall re-elevate the mountain as they belittle the achievement of the tallyman. (It is fitting to record that in China porcelain models of mountains were treasured, bringing dignity, tranquility and good fellowship to the gastronomic landscape of the table.)

From the Outer Hebrides

Andy Goldsworthy is a natural magician. With nothing up his sleeves but his inventive arms, he uses natural materials to construct objects and patterns which are generally ephemeral and often winningly decorative. He plays along with Nature until it reveals its nature. When the idea of the form catches the nature of the material, the delight that flares is like the pleasure in seeing a puzzle elegantly solved when we didn't even realise that there was a puzzle. A box whose sides are sycamore leaves, pinned with thorns, displays the architectural strengths of a leaf that I doubt we greatly attend to, summer or autumn. A cairn of stones brings to order the dispersed spectrum on the beach, as though the work had run entropy backwards: no longer fragments of an aggregate, beach stones become available to us in a new way, in new relationships. And pebble marks pebble, rock splits rock: this nature of pebbles is transformed into and expressed by a spiral of progressively sized pieces, their division a dark backbone that reminds me equally of fossils and reptiles, archaic images.

Whether conspicuous or left discreetly beneath a bush, Goldsworthy's work inhabits a world in which his good-natured alterations to place and form instruct us in appreciation of and genial accommodation to the transience of things.

Beach Cairn, 1985
Collected pebbles, St.Abb's, The Borders

54 Andy Goldsworthy
Broken Pebbles, 1985
Scratched white with another stone, St Abb's, The Borders

Large fallen oak tree. Used leaves with twigs still
attached to make supporting structure inside ball.
Wind, cloud, sun, rain. Jenny Noble's Gill, Langholm, 1985

Emerging from the grey... words lock, lace and brace not to straitjacket experience but to liberate it. David Tremlett enjoys travelling, and wherever he aims for he seems to wind up relishing the tang of a border life, animated by the criss-crossing of cultural currents. As with the hybrid musics he so enjoys (from Highlife to Cajun), so with the cultural landscapes in which he finds himself: life, like dance music, is to be lived not contemplated (a sure way to misunderstandings), and the rhythms of place are there to set the foot tapping. Tuning in to where you are, Tremlett believes, involves being open to possibilities as they arise. (Thus he shows an affinity to the urbane surrealists, such as the Breton of *Nadja,* with their concept of *disponibilité,* an availability to chance events, an ever-readiness to take up the revealed dispositions of situation and circumstance. To live driven by an imperative aye for the main chance, however, is itself a form of unfreedom, as Sartre pointed out. The only comfortable compromise is to so arrange things that you always win by accident.)

Just Lucifer disarrays a number of overheard remarks. They have an oracular significance, perhaps, the recurrent crux of the matter inviting divinatory interpretation. Better: here is notated the groundplan of a dance of serendipity. An idea takes a man for a waltz.

David Tremlett
Just Lucifer, 1985

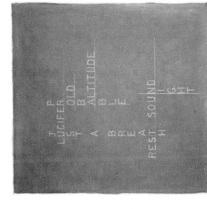

The work of art, suggested Benjamin, is the death mask of its conception. However in the event the action goes beyond its intended resting place, just as the thrown stone never merely marks the water's surface but sends radiating ripples to lick the bounding margin. *Pine:* the ghost traces of bits of trees seem penned beneath the mesh of discontinuity between sheet and sheet edge to edge, regular as the plots in a cemetery. Each twig and leaf has its presence inscribed as a shaping of density, a destiny impressed into the work by Linda Taylor's careful preparation. This elegy is at once a hoarding; all ideographic writings resemble the fossil record, in that they contain within themselves many of the most ancient plant drawings. Nowadays, only 12 per cent of Scotland's surface is wooded, and without due respect and care we shall fell the future.

In the next century
or the one beyond that
They say,
are valleys, pastures,
We can meet there in peace
if we make it.

To climb the coming crests
one word to you, to
you and your children:
Stay together
learn the flowers
go light

from *'For the Children'*, Gary Snyder

Herman de Vries wishes his art to bypass appearance and access actuality. The stuff of the world is immediate, and that which is there (whatever our conceptual and emotional prejudices might avow) is there as the ground of all, and not just human, existence. In actuality, there is a primordial ecology of natural relations which resists analysis, being composed of processes of becoming in mutual relationship and interaction: there is no time as clocks aim to follow because there is no stasis that can mark time, no interruption or tick in the flux. The primary task must be to re-immerse oneself in reality, to regain an assurance of unity.

An insistence upon the natural unity of all things is a consistent theme in human thought, sounding like a tinnitus in the inner ear of all contemplatives. It founds a worldview that was viciously suppressed as sorcery in the West, but which re-emerges, inflected with Eastern thought, in the philosophies of deep ecology and the concepts of Gaia, as well as in a fashionable nostalgia for the occult. De Vries sees the artist's task as one of promoting in a social context a 'becoming aware' of actuality. He has dramatised his dependence on the plant world by ingesting it in great variety: 'I am what I consume'. He attempts to present the material of the world as directly as possible: thus, he presents it inevitably as a transformation, pointing up the process of his art – for example, drying, rubbing. The world is, for him as it was for Paracelsus, a text, legible to all who will read without the divisive bifocals of language. And he is the world, for he identifies with the world in full mutuality.

When in Scotland during the summer of 1986, he was moved by the experience of finding a forest named on his map, but no forest being there when he went to that place. Sadly, words are a poor guide to reality. On the other hand, *From Scottish Earth,* a panel of earth rubbings, is a kind of magic square, such as Klee would have understood.

herman de vries from the shore of loch dughaill, 1986

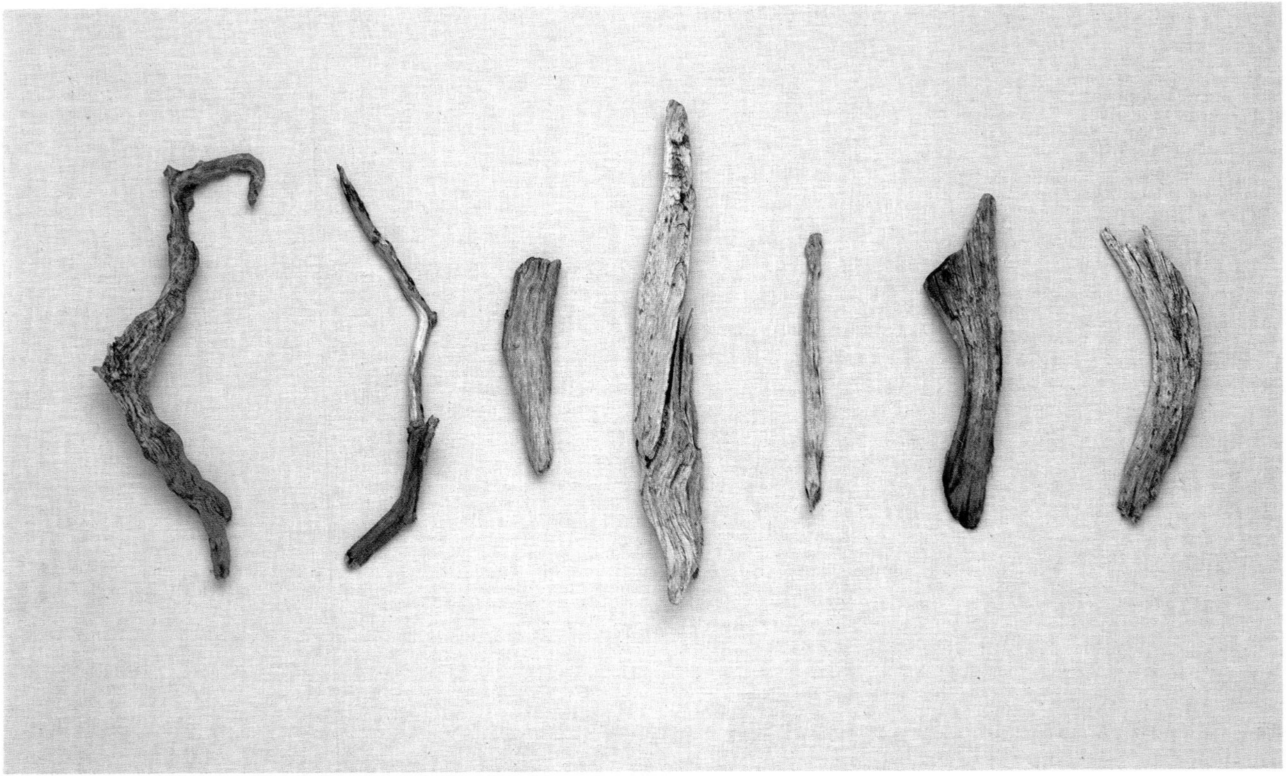

62 **herman de vries**
from scottish earth, 1986

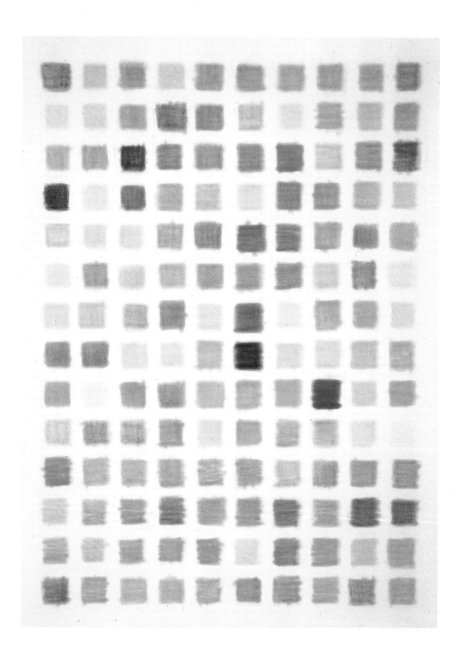

1. gorebridge
2. moorfoot hills
3. moorfoot hills
4. moorfoot hills
5. whitehope
6. whitehope
7. romanno bridge
8. romanno bridge
9. forth
10. whitburn
11. lanrick castle
12. loch earn
13. loch earn
14. loch earn
15. killin
16. glen dochart
17. glen dochart
18. glen dochart
19. glen dochart
20. glen dochart
21. glen dochart
22. glen dochart
23. strath fillan
24. strath fillan
25. strath fillan
26. strath fillan
27. strath fillan
28. strath fillan
29. glen coe
30. glen coe
31. onich
32. loch linnhe
33. loch linnhe
34. loch linnhe
35. fort william
36. leacann doire bainneir

37. leacann doire bainneir
38. invergarry
39. loch garry
40. loch garry
41. beinneun forest
42. beinneun forest
43. bunloinn forest
44. bunloinn forest
45. loch cluanie
46. loch cluanie
47. loch cluanie
48. shiel bridge
49. inverinate
50. allt glean udalain
51. allt glean udalain
52. allt glean udalain
53. allt glean udalain
54. strathcarron
55. loch kishorn
56. loch kishorn
57. loch kishorn
58. loch kishorn
59. loch kishorn
60. loch kishorn
61. loch kishorn
62. loch kishorn
63. glenshieldaig forest
64. glenshieldaig forest
65. glenshieldaig forest
66. glenshieldaig forest
67. glenshieldaig forest
68. loch dughaill
69. balgy
70. balgy
71. balgy
72. balgy

73. glen torridon
74. coille na glas
    leitire-beinn eighe
75. coille na glas
    leitire-beinn eighe
76. loch maree
77. meall a'ghlubhais-beinn eighe
78. meall a'ghlubhais-beinn eighe
79. meall a'ghlubhais/ruadh
    stagbeag
80. eilean subhainn
81. anacaun
82. anacaun
83. anacaun
84. loch maree
85. loch maree
86. loch maree
87. loch maree
88. loch maree
89. loch maree
90. loch bad an sgalaig
91. loch bad an sgalaig
92. loch bad an sgalaig
93. loch bad an sgalaig
94. river kelly
95. river kelly
96. river kelly
97. inverewe gardens
98. meall snil a chrotha
99. croft hill-poolewe
100. coille na glas leitire
101. coille na glas leitire
102. coille na glas leitire
103. coille na glas leitire
104. coille na glas leitire
105. coille na glas leitire

106. gairloch
107. glen docharty
108. glen docharty
109. glen docharty
110. glen docharty
111. achanalt
112. achanalt
113. loch luichard
114. loch luichard
115. loch luichard
116. loch luichard
117. loch luichard
118. loch luichard
119. brahan
120. carrbridge
121. carrbridge
122. carrbridge
123. coylum bridge
124. auchgorish
125. auchgorish
126. auchogorish
127. auchogorish
128. loch carron/ardarach
129. strathcarron
130. aundorach
131. aundorach
132. newtonmore
133. newtonmore
134. drumochter summit
135. glen garry
136. glen garry
137. calvine
138. calvine
139. struan
140. struan

The poetic vision renders the world transparent, said Novalis, and later artists confirm the aspiration to and possibility of such a state in writings such as: 'I am beginning more and more to see behind, or, to put it better, *through* things' (Franz Marc).

Thomas Joshua Cooper's photographs invite us to collude in giving credibility to an illusion. An ice-scoured and rock-strewn sweep of land on Skye: it is cold, the boulders sparkle with snow and ice, clinging as snug as lichen. Through the earth pulses a soft and luminous light, the ground becomes a shroud of radiant haze. It is as if the surface of the earth has become transparent, and the insubstantiality of what is taken for the material world is revealed. There is a hush of expectancy: this is a place where things are coming to pass. A sense of blessing, and of a beginning.

Here (at last) is an image that can serve as metaphor for the Australian Aborigines' perception of the Dreaming, that already always present origin of the world which is marked by law and yearning. This is an elemental, primordial scene: here I suffer the quiet force of the possible. Anxiously, I am home.

An apparent transfiguration re-enchants the world, and I am returned to a sense of my time as an architecture of possibility. The poetic vision offers us not knowledge, but an intensification of what we already knew.

THOMAS JOSHUA COOPER

barren and flawed
Boulder Field, The Storr
Isle of Skye
Scotland, 1986

'Dreaming the Old Man'

barra

flawed

Alienated from nature we are split off from ourselves, for we are a part of nature, there is a natural in and for us. The domination of the natural world – most clearly seen in the commercial exploitation of irreplaceable natural resources – expresses a fundamental desire to dominate ourselves, both collectively and singly. We exercise ourselves to expel and nullify a human nature which we commonly construe as an otherness, whilst striving to cultivate a second nature that connives in our oppression.

Shamanistic beliefs, which demand a radical acknowledgement of the integrity of all nature, thrive because they are so pervasively denied. Searching for a sense of identity which involves being at home in the world, the realms of nature (and of dreams) are not disconnected signs to the shaman, but possess a real and originary relationship to the self. The inner being and the outer domains are no longer separated, and a journey in the one is a journey in the other also.

Chris Drury's art relates him to personally significant objects and events in nature. It involves a practice that in essence requires solitude, calm and quietness: 'I have searched in the darkness, being silent in the great lonely stillness of the dark', said Najagnag, an Inuit shaman, speaking of the conditions for acquiring wisdom. The object is to see the object.

Four spheres strike chords of resemblance, of scales and of kinds. The shoulder blade of a caribou, cracked in the heat of the fire, is raised and aligned with the Alaskan horizon. It indicates where the caribou are to be found.

Deer Scats, Deer Bones, Pine Cones, Pine Bones, 1985

A displaced, dispossessed and disinherited people sometimes blames its fallen state on the loss of texts, of literacy itself. So the Ainu. The refugee White Hmong are trying to repair their loss – having reinvented their writing they have written afresh their basic texts, and are sure they will recover their full power once they are able to read them.

Ian Hamilton Finlay diagnoses in us an alienation from our own culture. The language we use is askew and our thought no longer squares with our history. His art comes 'like a thunderclap upon the conscience' (as was once said of John Wesley's teaching) to remind us that art is an ethical practice, pervading the whole of life, and rooted in history. The historical allusions, precisely drilled and deployed in his work, valorise history as a tale with a moral import: we can learn from history. Ignore or deny the presence of the past (thrown by what happened, they die cast by actuality) and the telling quotation becomes sloganising, and the teasing reference that demands that erudition be deployed in interpretation shifts its weight from a Santayanan reclamation of the amnesiac's past to a provocative attempt to impose a contested political corpus.

Despite a persistent neoclassicism, it is not the neoclassical tenor of Finlay's work that provides its salutary subversive moment. Reference to the ideals of classical art can for us play the same role as the intervention – or the appeal for the intervention – of a god in Greek tragedy; it can provide for the disclosure of incoherence in moral standards and language. Nonetheless, however welcome each opportunity to muster our contempt for the divorce of morality and action characteristically proclaimed in the prevailing managerialist ethos, we must never forget that the supreme value of the integral life was articulated in a society which is practice denied any possibility of its realisation to most of its people: classical philosophy and art is silent about its debt to slavery and the subjugation of women. Finlay's art reinvigorates our moral purposiveness through provoking the question: can the values of the rational and just life to which neoclassicism alludes be instituted in the absence of repression? Such musings are commonly dismissed as merely ponderously dull, but the irrepressible invention and wit, the semiotic ricochet, of Finlay's work that compels our serious reflection – that, and the scrupulous life which refuses to compromise its artistic (and thus social, not merely civic) integrity despite the stentorian vacuities of our bureaucrats. (Nowadays terror issues from the office, and its agent is unreasoning compliance. It is the *form* of the unthinking, reflex, commodified response, never quite up to its own puffs, that so enrages the committed personality.) Each work stands as a redoubt in the Little Sparta campaign.

'*Revolution, n.*' discloses the seeds of revolution *in memoriam* yet ready to germinate in my own back garden. There is a lectern on hand, the prop of authoritative discourse ready to relay the lessons of history and divine the condition of the present, to mediate between *germ* and *spectator*. (Behind the classical impedimenta lies a pagan ritual of blood sacrifice to bring fertility: is the hieratic lectern – for the keeper and giver of the word, but rarely for the word given and the word kept – itself to be toppled?)

There is an extensive web of traditions that seek to capture the essence of humanity in the emblematic garden: gardens are good to think. The cultivated garden cultivates the gardener, and even the smallest but conscientiously tended plot may become ripe with the continuing possibility of Arcadia. But must society succumb to the blade again? I would like to think that the spectre of a return of Terror – a form of the sublime – is presented ironically, as providing an obstacle to our freedom which indeed we exercise in the overcoming of it. (I hanker for those other gardens: fragile and fugitive, lurking below gratings of abandoned coal chutes and sprouting like wart-hairs from the tops of walls. Growth that is rank, untidy, invasive and unplanned is hearteningly independent, cheeky and chirpy in finding its niche. The ordered garden which is itself unexpected is too often dedicated to eradicating the unexpected, and it is the garden which claims our pleasure and instruction, not the gardening: the formal garden seems to aspire to the condition of the untended garden. I hope to not always see the garden through the slit of a tank, nor consider the only significance in an untidy border to be the difficulty of getting the staff – or the time – to do things properly these days.)

Finlay declares the lived indivisibility of life. Creative work is an ethical and political practice, responding to the conditions which surround it and the aspirations it embodies. His work, his battles, and his garden are his word and his signature in the cultural landscape.

Revolution, n. 1986

REVOLUTION, *n.* a scheme for the improving of a country; a scheme for realising the capabilities of a country. A return. A restoration. A renewal.

The French REVOLUTION is but the forerunner of another, much greater, much more solemn REVOLUTION, which will be the final one.

Sylvain Maréchal

The REVOLUTION must not be confounded with *REVOLUTIONS.*

Jules Claretie

Presentiment – is that long shadow – on the Lawn –
Indicative that Suns go down –
The Notice to the startled Grass
That Darkness – is about to pass –
Emily Dickinson

The future is our sun, history our shade and our shadow. In the dark light of a solar eclipse in January 1889 Wovoka, a prophet-dreamer of the Northern Paiute, had a vision in which he received reassurance that the dead would return to help oust the Europeans and restore the Indian way of life. The white traders' liquor had promoted an intoxication that both bound the Indian into market relations in an attempt to satisfy a seemingly insatiable demand, and loosened cultural restraints against overhunting. Wovoka sought to cut the bonds to the settlers with an ecstatic round dance that would speed the arrival of the army of the dead. The Ghost Dance focussed the consciousness of a people on the strength of a way of life which, as it happened, was easily broken. The ghost shirts the Indian warriors wore to make them invincible in battle (as though it was they who had already enlisted in the ranks of their ancestors) failed to prevent, and probably facilitated, the massacre at Wounded Knee, the decisive and horrifying defeat of the 'Sioux' Nation. Most Indian peoples were not militarily conquered, however, but economically incorporated. More recently, there has been a resurgence of Indian 'consciousness', and the old ways are held to have the power to restore a fulfilling and harmonious relationship between human being and the rest of nature. The Ghost Dance revives.

The past is our sun, the future is our shadow.

Slowly with fluttering step as if wanting mass the sun's image tracks a record of concentration across the fissured surface of a piece of wood. The wood, found, string in place, by a Scottish loch, is of no significance, least of all in having no significance. Now is the lens of my life: Roger Ackling's burning glass welds wood, person, place and time in a flux of light. The wood is now, and through it I (for I am him) know myself in the world. With intense clarity I see that nothing has changed. No further strings are attached. Take it or leave it: wonderful.

A leaf of grass is the journey work of the stars.

(November morning: my breath blooms; each tree is left its white shadow on the field).

Roger Ackling
Opposite: Rannoch Moor, 1985, *actual size*
pp 78-79 *two-thirds actual size*

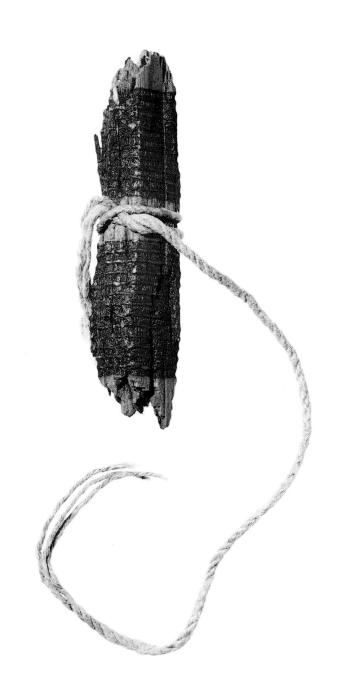

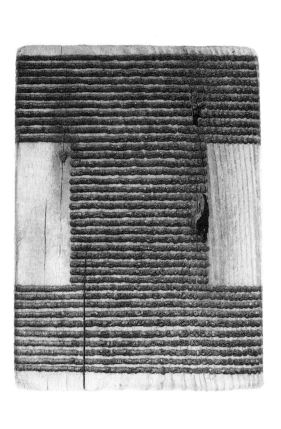

Richard Long works in both hemispheres. In a work which feints towards our glib separation of the subjective and the objective, the inner and the outer experience, the poetic and the rational, Long draws us on to a realisation – not of the need to overcome the classical separation of subject and object – but of the actual annihilation of the distinction in the constitution of actual experience attended to with a clear head. The column of place names marches like General Roy's surveyors across the landscape: but this path does not speak of the imposition of a rational path upon the land, rather it lies with all the determination of a discarded loop of string (:yet his walking was not inattentive.) This list is neither inventory nor itinerary, but a litany of landmarks, calling out natural features which have been associated with human history, human whim and folly, human interest. The names on the map and on our breath recall a past people intimate with the land: where there are fields, every field has its name. The 'objective' map is a social inscription of the apparently personal. To walk in a named place is generally to walk where others have gone before.

(And now for Long this unspectacular area near Blair Athol is marked in a way that can be passed on to his children, with the formula: 'Here is where...' I was watched by a deer, found an eggshell, saw a hen ptarmigan do the 'broken wing' display.)

(Here is where I lost my shadow in the mist.)

In the landscape as it registers in the mind perceptions, plans, sensations, art and steps are jumbled in a pot-pourri of time and image, the textured memory of place. The possibilities of naming arose in the condensations of experience. The leaves of history drip with that fusion of present absence that we call 'the past'. The mind map (already part of itself) arises like a mist from the ground of our life. But, no mistake, this map is a taking up of what is, its elements are objective, and they can be turned over to the public (they have that face, too). These things were.

There is a pair of stone masks which was made and used by the Tsimshian of the North-West Coast of America. They are identical, except that one is sightless, the other has staring holes for our eyes. It is as if one of these twins possessed outer vision, the other saw inwardly: seeing and imagining, sight and memory. The sighted mask fits exactly inside the blind: in a doubling back of self recognition, they are equally mirrors, equally masks. The landscape of consciousness forms at the interface.

TEN DAYS WALKING AND SLEEPING ON NATURAL GROUND

A 134 MILE MEANDERING WALK

SCOTLAND 1986

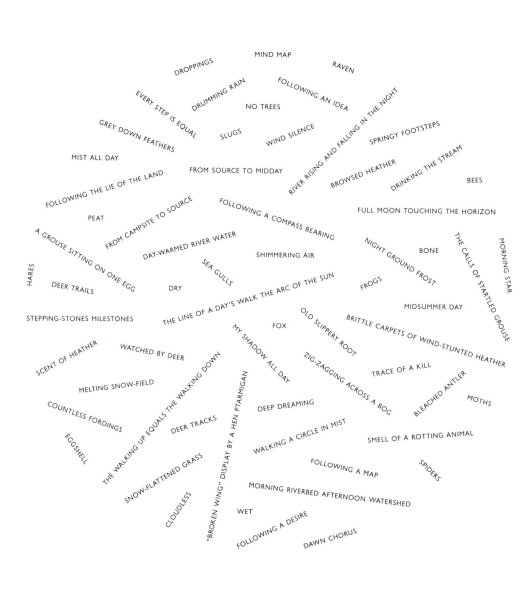

BEINN A'CHAIT
BEINN DEARG
ELRIG'IC AN TOISICH
BEINN GHARBH
BEINN BHREAC
AN SLIGEARNACH
MEALL ODHAR
ALLT DAMH DUBH
LEATHAD AN TAOBHAIN
CARN AN FHÌDLEIR LORGAIDH
SRÒN NA BAN-RIGH
CAOCHAN DUBH
RIVER FESHIE
ALLT A'CHAORAINN
SCARSOCH BHEAG
CNAPAN GARBH
BYNACK BURN
BRÀIGH COIRE CAOCHAN NAN LAOGH
CARN GREANNACH
AN SCARSOCH
SRÒN NA MACRANAICH
ALLT A'CHAORAINN
LEACHDANN FÉITH SEASGACHAIN
CARN EALAR
MEALL TIONAIL
GLAS FÉITH BHEAG
SRÒN GHARBH
GLAS FÉITH MHÓR
MEALL TIONAIL NA BEINNE BRICE
LOCH MHAIRC
CARN A'CHIARAIDH
BEINN MHEADHONACH
FÉITH AN LOCHAIN
AONACH NA CLOICHE MÓIRE
BRÀIGH NAN CREAGAN BREAC
BRÀIGH CLAIS DAIMH
CARN A'CHLAMAIN
BRÀIGH SRÒN GHORM
SRÒN DUBH
MEALL DUBH-CHLAIS
TARF WATER
FÉITH UAINE MHÓR
MEALL TIONAIL
CONLACH MHÓR
BRÀIGH COIRE NA CONLAICH
AN SLIGEARNACH
TARF WATER
CNAPAN NAN LAOGH
AN SGARSOCH
BYNACK BURN
CNAPAN GARBH
SCARSOCH BHEAG
ALLT A'CHAORAINN
MEALL TIONAIL
RIVER FESHIE
LEATHAD AN TAOBHAIN
CARN EALAR
LEACHDANN FÉITH SEASGACHAIN
BRÀIGH SRÒN GHORM
AONACH NA CLOICHE MÓIRE
CARN A'CHLAMAIN
BRÀIGH NAN CREAGAN BREAC
FÉITH AN LOCHAIN
BEINN MHEADHONACH
CARN A'CHIARAIDH
ELRIG'IC AN TOISICH
BEINN DEARG
BEINN BHREAC
BEINN DEARG
BEINN A'CHAIT

a dust of events
in a slender horizon of words

leaves
of absence

(out of horizons
I make a hammock)

Waiting on the ledge of night; then at dawn a man's shadow skims across the earth's surface to form a silhouette in space. A moment later it shrinks, lying like a dark omen across the landscape. Hamish Fulton's shadow accompanies those of the rocks that lie scattered on the flat summit of Ben Macdui. There seems to be a halo around that head lying metres away (an optical illusion due to contrast? an effect of the diffraction of light? an idiosyncracy of the photographic print?) and this reinforces the impression that the stones are at prayer. All these shadows converge (as they must) on the vanishing point at the horizon, an imaginary double of the sun, an absent twin of the sun that counterpoints the absent body of the artist. I stand in his stead: I am the double of his ghostly presence. The bodily gnomen indicates West, and beyond the ringing horizon lies (O my America! my new-found-land..) another place that this shadow cannot touch. The shadows compose an image of time and place and of the artist present in this place: but nothing has been disturbed, all will be as it was tomorrow morning. The rocks rest. Here is a place of rock, not people. It is as it is.

('Then I was standing on the highest mountain of them all, and round about beneath me was the whole hoop of the world and while I stood there I saw more than I can tell and I understood more than I saw, for I was seeing in a sacred manner the shapes of things in the spirit, and the shape of all shapes as they must live together like one being... And I saw that it was holy'. Black Elk's vision as he stood at the summit of Harney Peak is in the spirit of Fulton's work.)

The shadow lies on the ground like the memory of a past walk. (Close your eyes the better to retrace your footsteps: the old woman's arm wavers, then finds the direction of the dreaming track.) The landscape is a palimpsest of journeys, a

W I N T E R

N I G H T S

SOLSTICE SUNRISE ON BEN MACDUI A SEVEN DAY CIRCULAR WALK CAIRNGORMS SCOTLAND JUNE FULL MOON 1986

A THREE DAY WALK BY WAY OF BEN MACDUI SUMMIT OCTOBER FULL MOON 1986
SEVEN DAYS WALKING AND SEVEN NIGHTS CAMPING IN A WOOD CAIRNGORMS MARCH 1985
A WALK FROM THE SUMMIT OF BEN NEVIS TO THE SUMMIT OF BEN MACDUI MIDSUMMER 1975

text (a weaving) of ancestral lives. It would be good to have one's purpose: to leave the world so that others may come and go, may find themselves and the world in their wandering. Hamish Fulton has made eight connecting walks in Scotland: the landscape is beginning to know him.

Knowing a landscape takes time, the rhythm of simple activity, and a mind uncluttered with the anxious chatter of thought. (Silence is, for us, the sign of language's fulfillment: consequently, words used straightforwardly, lifted in the silence – in Fulton's texts – these seem enigmatic, almost paradoxical.) 'To learn to see, to learn to hear, you must do this – go into the wilderness alone', said Matsuwa, a Mexican Huicho shaman. 'Such things are learned only in solitude.' The result is the mysticism of things that cannot be put into words, of things that can only manifest themselves, with which Wittgenstein lassoed the sense of the world. Only in silence can you stumble upon a fawn or hear the frost crackle in the rock. This mystical intuition is not a romanticism, but a just recognition of participation in Nature. In a profound sense, my existence is tolerated on this planet only so long as I tolerate, through it, myself. Hamish Fulton's art is founded on a morality of radical humility and deep respect towards all of the natural world. His landscape art represents things as they are, freed of our desire, our will and domination. Destroying the natural world, intervening in the few remaining wildernesses, puts us all in jeopardy.

A Haida creation myth has Raven's grandfather saying to Raven:

'I am you. That is you.'

Stop chattering: let's eavesdrop some more.

Each thing has its own song.

The nun Shidò, founder of the Tòkeiji convent-temple in the thirteenth century, wrote:

If the mind does not rest on anything, there is no clouding,

And talk of polishing is but a fancy.

If the mind does not rest on anything, how will anything be seen or heard or known or understood?

Rising and sinking according to the current,

Going and coming, no footprint remains.

Same problem: how every philosophy is language and nonetheless consists in rediscovering silence.

Merleau-Ponty, October 22, 1959

It is impossible to mention all the sources which have stimulated the ideas and arguments of these essays, but I would be negligent if I failed to note the following works, which have been constantly by my side:

M. Merleau-Ponty: *The Visible and the Invisible,* Northwestern University Press, 1968; T. Legging:*The Warrior Koans,* Arkana, 1985; T.W. Adorno: *Aesthetic Theory,* Routledge & Kegan Paul, 1984 (1970); W. Benjamin:*One-way Street,* New Left Books, 1979; SRT Project:*While the Earth Endures,* Church of Scotland, 1986; S. Beckett:*Ill Seen, Ill Said,* Calder, 1983; W. Duff: *Stone: Images: B.C.,* Oxford University Press, Toronto, 1975; K. Thomas: *Man and the Natural World,* Allen Lane, 1983.

The artists contributing to *The Unpainted Landscape* have been generous beyond any reasonable expectation. My discussions with them have enriched my life immeasurably. However, they are in no way to blame for the curious arguments and perverse comments in which my text abounds: they are my wilful doing alone. I most especially thank Gill Reason and my friends Hamish and Nancy Fulton and Roger Cardinal, scrupulously honest in all they say, who suffered my argument (both tentative and passionately dogmatic!) with exemplary forbearance. James Bustard, Simon Cutts and Graeme Murray provided me with every facility for developing my text, nurtured it (and me) with unflagging enthusiasm and sympathy, and at the end juggled the roles of indulgent uncle and wicked step-mother with a dexterity that ensured this essay was delivered, if not on time, then at all! Finally, Carol, Katy and Maz: without whom...

David Reason
Canterbury
November 1986

'Nature Knows Nothing Of What We Call Landscape'

Jonathan Williams

Diogenes of Sinope, we are told, went around Athens in the third century BC (inside a barrel, armed with a lantern), looking for an honest man. I don't understand. Was there as little light in Greece in those days as there is in the Uplands of Britain at the moment? Has the Kakistocracy turned down the voltage?

'A good man is hard to find,' said Diogenes, the old Cynic the Athenians called 'The Dog'. The late Mae West – whose homefires were always lit and burning – improves on Diogenes by remarking: 'A hard man is good to find.' When it comes to landscape, the photographers Raymond Moore and Thomas Joshua Cooper agree with her. Another way of putting it: 'There is nothing in nature that is not in us.' The sculptor Naum Gabo said this.

A decade ago I wrote a piece for an exhibition catalogue at the Victoria & Albert Museum called *The Land,* 20th century landscape photographs selected by Bill Brandt. The temptation might be to add a few tatties and re-fry the whole mess. It was kaleidoscopic in the extreme, with the poet seldom sticking to one thing for five sentences, as he pursued his paratactic, peripatetic, cathectic way. Ten years after that piece, titled 'Some Speak of a Return to Nature – I Wonder Where They Could Have Been?' (a witticism of the cosmic order first uttered by the photographer Federick Sommer), I have slowed the pace. I am much more interested in Plainness and Dumbness. We are all in luck!

L A N D S C A P E – write it big. And then go to the *Oxford English Dictionary* and see if there are any micro-chaps lying about to plug into the system. Yes, there are:

> A. Stafford, *Fem. Glory* (1635): 'As terrible to them as a Lanscippe with a May-pole in it.'

A. Gibson's 'L'Envoy' in *Guillim's Heraldry* (1660): 'As in a curious Lant-schape, oft we see Nature so follow'd, as we think it's she.'

Norris, *Pract. Disc.* (1698): 'Nothing which this visible World can set before us is worthy our regard, especially when at the End of the Landskip, the Invisible Glories of Heaven Solicit and Court our Love.'

Watts, *Logic* (1725): 'As a Painter who professes to draw a fair and distinct Landskip in the Twilight, when he can hardly distinguish a House from a Tree.'

Emerson, in his *Essays* (1841): 'In landscapes, the painter should give the suggestion of a fairer creation than we know.'

Ruskin, *Modern Painters* (1844): 'The true ideal of landscape is precisely the same as that of the human form.'

Mozley, *Univ. Serm.* (1876): 'There are no two more different landscapes than the same under altered skies.'

Tennyson, *Ld. of Burleigh* (1882): 'He is but a landscape-painter, And a village maiden she.'

Anthony's Photogr. Bull. (1980): 'A fairly good camera and a single landscape lens...'

The usual rag-tag collection of Platonists and Calvinists and British intellectuals having great difficulty taking pleasure in the murky scenes in front of their cold noses. Mr Mozley's observation, however, is a sharp one; and John Ruskin dares to hint of comely goings-on in yon bosky dells. Witness: the thing I like best about staring out over the typewriter at the range of fells on the north flank of Lower Dentdale '(Long Rigg' on the map) is that it is uncannily sleeping on his right side. A male principle to align with the River Dee, sacred to a Celtic goddess, meandering by in the foreground.

Another item I look at across the valley is a cluster of Scotch pines in a field.

The light in Dendale is unusually dim and the pines are often inconspicuous and unremarkable. But, let the late sun shine its rays from the west up the dale – particularly in a month like October – and the trees become transfigured, with the forms of the foliage and those of the trunks and the elongated shadows endlessly fascinating to the eye. The air is as cool and palpable as amber. Everything is seen 'in a new light.'

'ONE LOVES ONLY FORM!' Charles Olson boldly declares that early in *The Maximum Poems.* It smacks of Herakleitos. I wish I knew who said it first. I wish Herakleitos could ramble with us on the Howgill Fells above Sedbergh in Cumbria – on the flank of Arant Haw, looking to Calders Rigg, Bram Rigg, and White Fell, the shapeliest hills in England. Would he have said 'Eyes and ears are poor informers to the barbarian mind'; or, 'There are gods here, too'?

To see it takes LIGHT. The Aryan root is *leuk-*, to shine, to be white. Cloud and dark over Britain have seen to that, so it is one of the amazing achievements of the best artists on these islands that they have done so much with an infinite range of greys. I now proclaim Raymond Moore as the Honorary President of the *Grey Liberation Movement,* and I put him up there with John Sell Cotman, whose fame stops at the North and Irish Seas apparently because he is too subtle for people in sun hats. I have a Pennine limerick in honour of Cotman:

> *Assessing the angle of Ingleborough*
> *caused Cotman to dangle his single bore*
> *in a glish bit of clay,*
> *mixed with Paine's grey,*
> *he kept in a monochrome shingle burrow.*

Riding yesterday to Leeds from Kirkby Stephen on the 'intensely scenic' Settle/Carlisle railway line, suddenly there was great Ingleborough Hill as you crossed the Batty Moss viaduct: pure Paine's grey, with a dollop of HP Sauce, rising over the immediate tangle of firewood, nettles, bindweed, and ragwort. (Curiosity about what there was to see in the immediate tangle would, of course, keep Mr Moore's and Mr Cooper's cameras pointed close to the ground, with hardly a nod to the familiar silhouette of the millstone-grit and limestone mountain.)

What I have been getting at is that some of us look at landscape as aesthetes and sensualists. If I had to farm up Dentdale (move the bull, milk and cows, dip the sheep, spread the muck, invite the heifers in for tea), I'd be on a plane tomorrow morning and never see the place again. Think of having to addle a living by repairing rood after rood of dry-stone walling. How much easier it is for us off-cumed uns to glory in the extravagant presence of these walls snaking over the fells. 'I just love Nature,' said the Yuppie girl friend of Guy Mendes, photographer in the Kentucky Blue Grass, 'but I don't want to get any on me.'

Having Ray Moore in the cottage at this instant, digesting his fishpie and samphire and Riesling, I'll ask him point-blank if anything I have written here so far makes any sense to his way of seeing. And, if he says yes, after that I want to ask him for a specific remark about each of his prints in this exhibition.

RM: 'The thing I like about what you're writing is that it's *lively*, something I'll want to read a few times. It's not like a letter from the bank manager; a 'critic' who's certain he knows more than you; or the Inland Revenue about what's wrong with one's financial balance and way of life in general... Here are the six prints in the show, grouped 1-2-3, with a space, and then 4-5-6:

(1) Ecclefechan, 1986: I get a lot of excitement out of the play of the light: the little group of flowers at the base of the wall, the menacing, cropped yew tree... the way the hill is divided by the tree, the wires making a kind of calligraphy, the bare trees over the wall, the flat areas, the broken hedge at the front – all conspiring to make an 'ambient magic', to go a bit portentous... Paul Nash was an early love. And much contemporary sculpture.

(2) Mallaig, 1985: Why shouldn't we be as interested in the little pile of wood, the old bath, the mystery of what's behind the back door, the odd light in the sky, the decorative fence as in gawking at the statue of a bloody cabinet minister on a bloody pedestal? (A lot of people think I'm a raving loony who ought to be locked up in a bothy in the Lake District and made to photograph Great Gable and Scafell twice a day until I got it right.)

(3) Campbeltown, 1985: Ordinary rotary clothes-line in the backs of some two-storey flats. At the particular moment they seemed like giant spider webs that had landed from Mars during the night. I like things 'taken' out of the mundane

and everyday. The man-made and the natural way thus take on a curious at-one-ment, an affinity to do with 'magic' and a transformation. The light – just at the moment – reveals a structural map of forms, of strange microcosmic architecture. People are often disappointed by such pictures, because they offer no visual pre-conceptions. They ride in on their isolation and ask: 'Why take a picture of that?' Yep. Lock him up.

(4) Dumfriesshire, 1985: Your quotation ('one loves only form') from Charles Olson seems very apt. The excitement – dare I say *beauty?* (I hate the bloody word!) – is in the coherence of forms. I nearly froze waiting for that bus to loom up out of the mist and work against the sign.

(5) Gigha, 1985: Here, again, the concrete structure with the iron grill, and the house appearing through the shed, as though there were a mirror there. The contrast with the grasses, and a house vaguely emerging in the foliage, and the fence line and the line of the wall crossing the field – areas of visual significance for a single instant. What odd luminosities are concentrated in the two buildings.

(6) Kintyre, 1985: A place for breeding fish. Yet, a world with which you feel a moment of 'affinity'. The light, *just then,* creates an atmosphere in which the forms are inviting. The reason for taking pictures is for the *excitement.* Painters know this. Photographers seldom do.'

Time to take a wee break. Read some Arthur Machen. Take a walk around the headland of Chaipaval on South Harris. A topic like *The Unpainted Landscape* would not have suited the late Clarence Schmidt of Woodstock, New York. The last time I saw him he was diligently painting every tree on his place with aluminium paint... One of Anton Bruckner's stranger activities was trying to count all the leaves on a particular tree as he sat in the Biergarten sinking a few Steins of Pilsner Urquell. (Much easier to paint than count.) Ok. Back to something 'entirely different.'

Thomas Joshua Cooper inhabits a darker world altogether than Raymond Moore's. The latter forms coherences with Schubert as 'Wanderer,' and with Rilke's: *'Everything beckons us to perceive it, Murmurs at every turn, 'Remember me'.'*

Cooper goes to Theodore Roethke for clarity: *'At first the visible obscures: Go where light is.'* He's a member in good standing of the Old West Coast Zarathustra Gang ('don't fire until you see the lights in their eyes!'), and in a flash he's used the word *chthonian* and you're shot out of the saddle.

There are people – I am not one of them – who read that a photographic print is titled 'Ritual Guardians (Messages to Narcissus)'; and they don't reach for their gun, they simply shut their eyes. A bit of charity to the poor photographer, please. We are at a time and in a country where photographers and poets have no real place, no currency, and little clout. The works themselves are covert operations of no use to the nation-state. The hapless makers of such objects are tolerated rather like monks with bad breath and psoriasis – at arm's length. Anyway, look past one's humble efforts to hook your attention. Thomas Joshua Cooper is the maker of some superb images. Witness: I love the photographs of Clarence John Laughlin, even though they have names like 'The Radiator As a Hand, The Headlight As a Gaping Fish.' (Are you trying to tell us something, Clarence?) I love the painting by Ivan Albright titled, god help us, 'Into the World Came a Soul Named Ida.' I even have a poem of my own called 'The Reverend Septimus Buss Meets the Great Norwegian Linguist Sophus Bugge On the Crags of Craig Yr Ysfa And Mutters About the Previous Day's Fishing in the Afon Llugwy Below the Swallow Falls.' All that follows is:

> *cowt*
>
> *nowt*
>
> *nobbut*
>
> *newts*

Give Cooper his dualistic world and his Castaneda and his animism and his Jung and his whatever. A photograph like 'Guardian Ghosting', from the beautifully produced book *Between Dark and Dark* (Graeme Murray, Edinburgh, 1985), makes me wonder if he knows the horror novels of his American contemporary, Peter Straub? I got *If You Could See Me Now* off the shelf the other evening and opened it at random to page 157. How odd: there was the passage I wanted:

'There was a darkening of the spirit. Going closer to where I had to go, I saw the edges of starlight on the bark-rills and began to be afraid. When I passed through a gap, it

seemed to close behind me. The breathing life of the forest expressed an immensity of force. Even the air grew tight. I climbed over a lightning-blasted trunk. Living stuff coiled around my boots, golden roots proliferated over them. I stepped on a mushroom the size of a sheep's head and felt it become jelly beneath my weight...

'*The trees jostled and whispered behind me. The blackness was edged and pierced by a thousand sharp silvery lights on leaf-edge and the curve of tendrils. The clearing was a dark circle at its center. I could move, and went forward. I touched the ashes. They were warm. I smelled wood-smoke, and it was heavy and sweet. The dense forest behind and before me seemed to grow taut. I froze beside the warm ashes, bent forward over my knees in a total silence.*'

Mr Straub's book is a frightening one. I have read it three times and haven't finished with it yet. Mr Cooper frightens as well. It is preternatural, how he is able to animate landscapes (Shropshire, Derbyshire, Scotland) that usually just look indistinct and stale – more shadows, more over-agricultural use, more gorse, more may, more dock, more ash. Gods from many cultures have walked these places. Some could yet. And he knows that the places remain sacred, in spite of all.

The work that Tom Cooper presents us with in *The Unpainted Landscape* is a complex one with six images, if I understand our telephone conversations. (We had hoped to meet in person in Glasgow or Dentdale, but the photographer has been suffering from re-current injuries from a fall while rambling on Skye.) The only part I have seen is what is in the book: two 20″ x 24″ prints in one mount. In the three-inch space between the prints, hand-written on the mount, are the words *barren and flawed*. On the back of the work prints I have in hand are further titles: 'Boulder Field, The Storr, Isle of Skye, Scotland, 1986'; and, 'Dreaming the Old Man.' God's teeth, sez this puzzled viewer, if a man puts not one nor two but three titles on a pair of related photographs, I say he has to go even further and spell it out. I don't see that I can tell you nothing more that is not full of cloudiness and adumbration. I can say that his images are remarkably airless, like the moon; that they suggest a Crimean battlefield hundreds of years after the event, that Cooper uses in '*flawed*' an accidental flare of light to brilliant effect, but this kind of description isn't the answer. (This paragraph is an insert written seven weeks after the rest. I begged TJC to put something down on paper. He said he was no writer. I said, *I'm* a writer, don't worry, I'll protect you from falling on your face, give us something flat, straight-out. He allowed that he was extremely pleased by the results of *'barren and flawed'* but the rest is silence. He said he was very cross with the British photographic establishment – who isn't – and thought more about sculptors like Richard Long and Hamish Fulton. Well, that's all I can ferret out. I'm leaving for North Carolina!)

Nothing beats the work itself, plus time and light and space in which to contemplate it. Voila. But, afore ye go, surely you'll not turn down another dram or two of Lagavulin and allow me to suggest another guide to the world of Thomas Joshua Cooper? that most genial and illuminating of phenomenologists, Gaston Bachelard. I love dipping into *The Poetics of Space* for his reveries on the world and what is beyond the world. The following is so on target: '...there exist numerous texts in which a meadow is a forest, and a tuft of grass a thicket. In one of Thomas Hardy's novels, a handful of moss is a pine wood; and in *Niels Lyne,* Jens Peter Jacobsen's novel of subtle passions (read and re-read by Rilke), the author, describing the Forest of Happiness, with its autumn leaves and the shadbush 'weighted down with red berries,' completes his picture with 'vigorous, thick moss that looked like pine trees or like palms.' Also, 'there was in addition, a thin moss that covered the tree-trunks and reminded one of the wheat-fields of elves.' ...This is one of the many daydreams that take us out of this world into another, and the novelist needed it to transport us into the region beyond the world 'that is the world of new love. People who are hurried by the affairs of men will not enter there.'

Enough gab. Pry your eyes open and look long and quiet at what Tom Cooper and Ray Moore have to show us. You'll need your wellingtons, a torch, a few jam-butties and nice tarts to offer Cernunnos, and some flexible twine with which to trace your steps home.

Paul-Armand Gette, Bernard Lassus, and an invisible person

Minimal Intervention

Lucius Burckhardt

'The Unpainted Landscape' is the landscape in our heads, formed through culture and education, which allows us to perceive the environment as a 'landscape' and give it significance. *'Minimal Intervention'* in landscape transforms it without the use of bulldozers and fertilizers, by changing our unpainted landscape so that we can find other meanings in the outer landscape.

There are two processes which construct it: the secular process of culture and that of individual development, which mirrors the cultural process in certain ways. This cultural process originates from the period when an urban population, freed from the daily labour of rural production, acquired a new aesthetic awareness of the surrounding countryside. This relatively new perception of the field as 'landscape' is so accepted, that we have difficulty in imagining anything else. But one can still observe these two cultures co-existing. For example, in a railway compartment crossing the alps, tourists will admire the landscape as picturesque whereas those who work on the land will question how it would be possible to make a livelihood in such terrain.

Friedrich Schiller remarked on this aesthetic awareness of landscape as a result of liberation from material constraints in his poem *'The Walk'*. Here the urban walker sees the 'happy tribe of the fields not yet awakened to freedom', as being a part of the landscape. However, he himself, having arrived at a state of consciousness in which he views the landscape as a place for leisure as well as work, remains distanced as a spectator. Similarly, the geography teacher at school presented us with the landscape of the Ruhr district, singling out smoking chimneys, hauling gear, and the miners returning from a shift in overalls and peaked caps, as being typical. 'Happy tribe...!

From this we can see that the use of the word landscape is a very complex one. On the one hand, it enables us to construct a unified image of the landscape from the multiple impressions that assail us. But, by the same token, we are imposing our selection of what we consider to be typical and atypical of an area – mines for the Ruhr, sheep for the Highlands. This leads in to the question of our reaction to the unexpected discovery of natural resources in an area where they do not coincide with our image of the place. Whilst preserving the hauling gear of the remaining Coal Age industrial landscape of the Ruhr (threatened by mineral oil), we might not allow hauling gear for mineral exploitation to be erected elsewhere. We can now see the ideological potentialities of the word 'landscape' for a man like Hitler and his landscape designer Alvin Seifert, who was responsible for the design of the German autobahns.

In feudal times, landscape was a term in common political usage, meaning the land belonging to a castle or town. In so far as these territories were represented by cartographers and classified by record-makers, the word became part of a specialist terminology. Then painters began to use the word in a more general sense, unrelated to a specific feudal unit, simply as a beautiful landscape. This aesthetic awareness was related to their knowledge of what had been developed in classical rhetoric and poetry, the topos of the charming place, *locus amoenus,* which forms the basic motif in early examples of pastoral poetry. The genre is that of *citysans,* urban people (of Athens and Rome) who have enslaved the last of the peasants. Happy tribe...!

The word was then adopted by travellers and later by tourists. They discovered 'landscapes' everywhere, which meant that during their travels they found places which corresponded to those they had previously seen in paintings or had elaborated in the imagination. Writers described or constructed landscapes which had an even greater element of the universal: these were seductive in that readers could easily combine them with their own 'unpainted landscapes'. An extreme example of this can be found at the beginning of *Wilhelm Meisters Wanderjahre,* where Goethe uses the literary device of reminding us of a familiar inventory, that of the Holy Family fleeing to Egypt, which we complement with our own re-invention of the scenery.

With the 'pictures' of authors, especially travel-writers, and memories of geography lessons, 'landscape' takes on a new meaning closer to the most ancient: landscapes are the defined places where we pass our holidays, landscapes are special. Landscape passes from the timeless, charming place to an object of fashion and aesthetic obsolescence. The history of tourism in the Alps can be seen as the discovery and expendability of landscape: in 1800 the big lakes, from 1840 the smaller ones nearer the mountains, followed by the waterfalls, then by the higher valleys, Davos, St. Moritz, followed by the glaciers, Bernina, Aletsch, the

Furka, and finally, by the end of the nineteenth century, only one more sensation was left to be enjoyed – the winter season.

The walk is the most interesting, and as yet not obsolete creator of landscapes; in our time it is frequently undertaken by car. The wonder of the trip lies in the transformation of a series of existing places into a unified image of an imaginary and conceptual landscape. A tourist visits Vézelay, the ruins of Cluny, takes in a sight at Beaune, samples some wine, and then, back at home knows 'what Burgundy looks like'. In this tourist's judgment the inhabitants have spoiled 'typical Burgundy', through an inability to recognise what is of intrinsic importance in their own landscape. The trip/walk, and the information gained from it, is the most affirmative sense of the 'unpainted landscape'. So now we can return to our initial subject, minimal intervention.

If we accept that landscape is not an object that exists, but is constructed by our culture and our minds, then this must obviously influence the art of gardening which is responsible for man-made landscapes. Today, the state of gardening is not as good as it has been, certainly if we judge it in relation to its official manifestations such as gardening festivals and exhibitions. This is the case, although there have never been greater means at its disposal, bulldozers, highly developed cultivations, the chemical power of fertilizers and herbicides. Problems caused by topography, soil or water-supply can be overcome, everything can be implemented, stagnant water at the top of a hill and arid scrub at the bottom, if the designer so wishes. At the German Federal horticultural exhibition, I saw azaleas in between grey prairie grass; and tulips in between Japanese miniature conifers. They looked like street-lamps in a forest. When all is possible, then means are used which destroy the sigificance of each other, and when there are no resulting effects, the designers feel obliged to reinforce the means....

Twice in the past, the art of gardening found itself in a cul-de-sac, and at both times, it was outsiders who gave it a new, decisive direction. Firstly, when English poets and dilletantes abandoned the French formal style and created the landscape garden; secondly when architects at the end of the nineteenth century abandoned the landscape garden convention in favour of the architectural garden. At the root of my argument on minimal intervention is the notion that there are now artists who will free gardening from its lost situation of maximal means. For minimal intervention has the characteristics of art, and therefore one's perception of the landscape is not produced directly, but is mediated through the means of a sign.

The landscape gardens of the eighteenth century were large enterprises, but were executed with principles, allied to those of minimal intervention. Lancelot Brown was given his nickname because he searched for places which had the potential or 'capability' of being transformed into what he imagined, whilst still retaining their original topography and vegetation.

In Germany, the transformation of the Wilhelmshöhe Park at Kassel from a Baroque garden into a landscape garden certainly involved major transportation of soil, but in spite of this was carried out with the means of minimal intervention. The Prince wanted the garden to be transformed without the destruction of his grandfather's work, a sequence of waterfalls crowned by a gigantic status of Hercules. The intervention consisted in the insertion of a 'gothic' castle in the upper left section, and the ruin of a Roman aqueduct in the lower section, to the right of the middle axis: so the famous S-shape was formed, and the Hercules Statue, without being touched, had become a garden folly among several others. The same transformation, in miniature, is repeated in the formal centre of the garden, a star of six radiating pathways in front of a grotto. Without intefering with the grotto, but with the introduction of water in an asymetrical S-shape, the new design appeals to the spectator's idea of nature as seemingly untouched.

All these eighteenth century installations contain the fundamental paradox of the landscape garden; landscape is represented by landscape. The mediative character of the symbol cannot be perceived as being separate from the direct impression of a natural, unaltered place. Indeed, research has revealed that the majority of visitors to the 'English Garden' in Munich, designed by Sckell, think that they are in a place which, though in the heart of the city, remains in its wild state. This direct representation of landscape by landscape is *not* a mode of expression of minimal intervention, which aims to affect the imagination of the spectator via a sign; in this respect, in its conscious use of artifice, minimal intervention has the character of art.

It was Bernard Lassus who discovered that the *'habitants-paysagistes'*, by means of this minimal intervention, lent an aspect of infinity to their gardens, in spite of the conditions of very restrictive plots of land. The superficial observer of middle-class education often sees nothing but the literal images: garden gnomes, miniaturised houses and castles, and fawns. However, the more imaginative

The Hercules Monument and the neo-gothic castle

102 **Bernard Lassus**
The Bridge over the Road
Parc des Salles, Istres near Marseilles

amongst the Suburban Landscapists do not use these images as such, but as symbols to convey distance and inter-relations: windmill and ship as signs of wide plains, the miniature buildings and surrounding plants to represent the transition from the man-made to nature.

In his own work, Lassus tries to utilise the example of the Suburban Landscapists, so that private symbols become signs which can be generally understood: the design of a public garden must necessarily refer to a common code of meaning. For Lassus, then, the greatest success is achieved, when his intervention – the artifice – becomes reality. I have seen garden-designers at the Stuttgart Federal Garden Exhibition put a water source on top of an artificial hill, which formed the roof of a covered highway: the water's relation with subsoil water streams was therefore implausible and the entire construction became an example of maximal intervention. Lassus, doing superficially the same thing, succeeds in transforming the false into the true. One of his projects was to design a bridge over an auto-route which bisects a public park. He constructed the bridge partly with the use of artificial rocks and placed a rural fountain on it. Whereas at Stuttgart, an attempt to create harmony in a despoiled situation resulted in gigantic artifice, the little, ironic mock fountain of Lassus has become a popular back-drop for local wedding photos: its falsification is accepted as reality because of its poetic character.

Ian Hamilton Finlay's garden works can also be seen as minimal intervention: it is self-evident that they are mediated by artistic symbols which they communicate through poetic inscriptions. By the means of this second medium, Ian Hamilton Finlay makes a direct reference to a cultural vocabulary. Through the inscription on a stone of *'See Poussin, Hear Lorrain'*, the pond of a Scottish croft is transformed into a scene from classical painting. The signature of Albrecht Dürer on a tablet in the grass evokes complex associations with *'The Great Piece of Turf'* at the Albertina, Vienna. By using these mediations, Ian Hamilton Finlay draws comparisons between things which are normally considered to be opposites: the garden and the woods; the pond and the sea; the tranquility of the 'charming place' and the battlefields of the Second World War; the virtues of the peasant and the virtues of the French Revolution. Finally Ian Hamilton Finlay's garden mediates on the relation between nature and the spectator. His inscriptions on tree trunks are allusions to both; to arcadian poetry and the motive of cutting one's name in the bark, and to inscriptions in a botanical garden and the labelling of nature – future attempts to appropriate nature in an anomic cultural situation.

The theme of science as a vain attempt to appropriate nature recurs in the minimal intervention of Paul-Armand Gette. His project for the botanical gardens of Basle involved the expansion of the cloud of little, enamel labels from the gardens to an adjacent hill: but all the labels indicated no other plant than *Plantago Lanceolata, L.*, the Ribwort-plantain. On the other hand, in his project *'Kassel - A Botanical Garden'*, he transformed the streets and open spaces of the town by labelling the weeds growing out of cracks in the pavements with Latin names. A recent 'minimal intervention', aimed at all the newly-built galleries of Europe, had landscape as its theme. Gette planned to install plastic waterlilies in the wash-basins of public toilets at these art galleries, and by using the inscription *Om* (zero meters) at the door, to pose the ironic question of where landscape begins. Unfortunately, only the Centre Georges Pompidou conceded to this complex installation with its allusions to a Monet landscape.

Through the extremes of minimal intervention, James Lee Byars interpreted an infinite landscape in the summer of 1983, but of course only in the minds of the spectators present. The performance, entitled *'A drop of black perfume'*, was staged in the grandiose landscape of meadows and rocks, punctuated by areas of melting snow, that forms the Furka. On one of the millions of rocks in the meadow, but carefully chosen before, Byars, vested with his golden robe and top hat, dropped a drop of synthetic perfume, in a performance which seemed to be as short as it was vain. A drop of perfume is nothing in an alpine air redolent with the smell of herbs and flowers. Yet, this intervention which lasted perhaps for a second, transformed the panoramic world of the Furka.

Joseph Beuys' legacy for Kassel *'7000 Oaks'* is certainly an art work on an ambitious scale; yet I would call it minimal intervention because it uses artistic means to communicate environmental issues. It informs that the constraints of politics and public order can be overcome by an outsider, the artist – and in fact, neither by force nor revolution, nor on the level of underground action and subversion, but through standard public processes. Beuys was invited by *Documenta 7* to erect a sculpture at Frederic Place, in front of the main Documenta building, the Museum Fridericianum. His sculpture consisted of 7000 blocks of basalt arranged in a long pile. In addition, Beuys declared that he would plant 7000 trees on public ground at Kassel, and that for each tree planted,

'Where is the beginning of the landscape?'
Kassel, 1985

106 **James Lee Byars**
A Drop of Black Perfume
The Furca, 1983

Planting one of the '7000 Oaks'

a block of basalt would be removed from the sculpture and placed beside it. The sculpture therefore consisted in its slow diminution, connected with the consciousness that whenever a stone was taken away, a tree would be planted in one of the town's districts. The completion of the sculpture consists in its complete absence, which informs us that the town of Kassel is now, in the words of Beuys, 'well-wooded' (which is play upon words; in German it sounds like 'administrated' – *verwaldet/verwaltet*).

The political purpose of Beuys' work starts from his assumption that a well-run town should have a garden department, whose policy would be to plant trees wherever it was physically possible. The concept of 7000 extra trees being planted by an artist was, for a municipality such as Kassel, absurd; it could not come to terms with the idea. However it could not refuse such a donation. The sculpture was already in place and the removal of the blocks of basalt would have reminded the citizens of Kassel that they had lost 7000 trees which Beuys might present to another town. Thus the administration had no alternative but to accept the bequest and supervise the planting itself, in order to avoid further scandals. It had to begin investigating 7000 tree sites that in official terms were supposedly non-existent.

Now to return briefly to gardens. It is definitely a very philistine approach to think that we can learn from art directly, but we can learn from this principle of 'mediated' expression, from minimal intervention. Both our most recent garden styles will soon arrive at the same old paradoxes. The neo-classical tendency is fallible in that it is synchronous with neo-classical architecture and this results in a rigid conformity between the styles of house and garden. The alternative of the ecological garden results in the same problems as the old landscaped garden.

Nature is invisible and cannot be represented directly, only by images. With our 500 or 1000 square metres of garden, we cannot hope to save a rare botanical species threatened by extinction, but we can symbolise the beauty of unencroached nature.

The Unsculptured Landscape

Lucius Burckhardt

Landscapes can only be reproduced in two-dimensional representations; the three-dimensional representation is possible in the 1:1 scale: by landscape-gardening. Reduced landscapes are folkloristic: Navivity cribs or Calvaria hills; or scientific; nineteenth century geographic reliefs or battlefield models. In high art landscape sculpture retired to the socles, reduced to the task of giving an allusion to the scenery of the representation.

But recently I found a landscape sculpture: an island. It is Italian maiolica; a specialist could localize it; for me it has something to do with the S. Chiara Cloisters at Naples. Astonishing is the manner of the representation: no miniaturized relief, but a combination of abstract and realistic informations. – Its function is to be a bonbonière.

The bonbonière is an island in the sea: the box is the sea, which is indicated by a blue ornament in the cartouches of the four sides, and the cover is the island, a regular, flat pyramid. On the four sides of the pyramid a realistic island is painted: four equal islands, consisting of a mountain and a promontory, probably hiding the port. – But how to get at the island? – It is quite easy: You open the bonbonière, and at the bottom of the box you will see the mountain and the promontory and the port formed by them. Closing the box is going on board a ship: You can see an island only from the sea – or be inside it.

Transients

A Selection made by Graeme Murray
from the School of Scottish Studies Photographic Archive

Mrs Stewart (cailleach), tinker. Lairg, Sutherland, 1957

Tinker's gellie, a beehive-shaped bough tent, covered mainly with tarpaulins. Situated near the old A9 outside Dalwhinnie, Inverness-shire, April 1986

The framework of a gellie about 150 yards from the main road.
White Sands, Morar, Inverness-shire, 1958

Colin Stewart, 'Taranty Auld Road' by Brechin, Angus, Easter 1982
Taranty Market was in former days much frequented by horse-dealing tinkers
and this encampment is at a traditional stopping place.

Peggy Stewart with the family's 'whirli', a two-wheeled barrow, with assorted gear such as a kettle, saw, etc. A 'pinky' or water drum hangs from a tree.
Lundin Links, Fife, November 1982

Tinker's encampment, Scouser looking to Glenuig, Skye, 1935
The government's policy as directed by the Secretary of State for Scotland is to end such haphazard camping and confine travellers to a network of sites.

Orðasafn

íslenzkt og enskt

A SHORTER

ICELANDIC TO ENGLISH

DICTIONARY

Abridged by Graeme Murray 1986
from Jón A. Hjaltalín's „Orðasafn"
Printed in Reykjavík 1883

A.

Á, n., river. Fs. on, upon.

áðan, atv., a short time ago.

aðdýpi, n., deep water close to the shore.

aðhjúkrun, n., attention, care, nursing.

aðhlæginn, l., given to laughing, fond of laughing.

afl, n., strength, power, might; virtue; validity; violence, force. Hearth (of a forge).

aflausn, n., absolution, remission of sins; release, discharge.

aflraun, n., trial of strength; bodily exercises.

afréttur, n., mountain pasture.

afskammta, s., allot, portion out.

aftök, n., excessively severe weather.

ágætur, l., excellent.

akuryrkja, n., agriculture, husbandry.

alda, n., wave.

aldin, n., fruit of trees.

aldingarður, n., fruitgarden, orchard.

aldur, n., age, life time, period.

áleiðis, atv., forward, onward; on the way.

aleiga, n., whole property.

algjöra, s., finish, perfect, complete.

allur, l., all, whole, entire.

almáttugur, l., almighty.

alþingi, n., Parliament, diet.

amstur, n., toil.

andi, n., breath; spirit.

andköf, n., gasping for breath.

andlát, n., death.

andlegur, l., spiritual.

andlit, n., face countenance.

andvaralaus, l., heedless, careless.

ánetjast, s., to be entangled (in a net).

annvirki, n., farmworks.

apturganga, n., ghost, apparition.

apturhaldsmaður, n., conservative.

árvakur, l., early rising.

áræði, n., courage, daring, pluck.

ásannast, s., prove true.

ásáttur, l., agreed upon.

ásetningur, n., purpose, design.

askur, n., ash, ash tree.

áskyna, l., aware of.

ás, n., beam, pole; yard. Rocky ridge.

ást, n., love.

ástúð, n., lovingkindness, love.

ástúðlegur, l., affectionate, loving.

atorka, n., energy.

átt, n., quarter of the horizon;

augabragð, n., twinkling of an eye, moment.

auðn, n., desert, wilderness.

B.

bardagi, n., battle.
beinn, l., straight; hospitable.
biðlund, n.,forbearance,patience.
birki, n., birch.
bjálki, n., beam.
bjalla, n., bell.
bjarmi, n., radiance.
blástjarna, n., blue star; Wega.

blíðskapur, n., mildness, kind-
    ness, friendly terms.
blíðviðri, n., mild weather.
blóðberg, n., thyme.
bogmaður, n., archer.
bókaskápur, n., press for books.
býfluga, n., bee.
bygg, n., barley.

D.

Dá, n., fainting fit.
dáð, n., deed; valour; strength.
dáðlaus, l., feeble, weak.
dagan, n., dawn, daybreak.
dagfar, n., conduct, daily life.
dagleið, n., day's journey.
dagsbrún, n., daybreak, dawn.
dagsetur, n., nightfall.
dagur, n., day.
dís, n., goddess.

djúp, n., depth; deep sea.
drápa, n., heroic poem.
draumur, n., dream.
dygð, n., virtue; integrity.
dæma, s., judge, pass sentence.
dögg, n., dew.
döggfall, n., dewfall.
djöfull, n., devil.
dökkblár, l., darkblue.

E.

eðli, n., nature.
egg, n., egg. Edge; ridge (of
    a mountain).
eik, n., oak; tree.
eikiviður, n., oakwood.
eilífð, n., eternity.
einstakur, l., famous, rare.
einvera, n., loneliness, solitude.
einvígi, n., single combat.
eiturormur, n., viper.

eldfjall, n., volcano.
eldgamall, l., very old.
eldglæringar, n., flakes of fire.
elgur, n., elk; halfmelted snow.
elskhugi, n., lover, sweetheart.
embætta, s., conduct divine ser-
    vice.
endurnæra, s., refresh, nourish.
enni, n., forehead; precipice.
epli, n., apple.

F.

Fá, s., get, obtain, gain, acquire;
fábyggður, l., thinly peopled;
fagur, l., fair, beautiful, fine.
fannkoma, n., fall of snow.
far, n., motion; ship; passage;
  footprints; disposition; condition; behaviour.
féhirsla, n., treasury.
feigð, n., approach of death.
fegurð, n., beauty.
féhirðir, n., shepherd; treasurer.
fenna, s., snow; be covered
  with snow.
ferð, n., travel, journey.
ferðabók, n., book of travels.
ferðamaður, n., traveller.
ferðbúinn, l., ready for a journey.
festing, n., firmament.
fjallagola, n., mountain breeze.
fjallasýn, n., mountain view.
fjarri, atv., far, far off.

fjársjóður, n., treasure.
fjarski, n., distance; immensity.
fjölga, s., increase the number
  of; become numerous.
fjölmenni, n., many people,
  crowd.
fleki, n., raft.
flóð, n., flood, inundation, de-
  luge.
forngripur, n., antiquity.
fornmenn, n., flt., ancients.
fors, n., rage, violence; waterfall.
framstafn, n., prow.
framvegis, atv., for the future.
framsýn, l., prophetic.
frost, n., frost.
frumvaxta, l., in prime of life.
fylking, n., battle array.
fyrirburður, n., vision.
fyrirfara, s., kill, destroy.
fönn, n., snowdrift.

G.

gagnaugu, n.flt., temples.
gagndrepa, l., wet through.
gjálfur, n., din, roar (of the sea);
  chatter.
glampa, s., gleam.
glóra, n., faint light, glimmer.
  S., glimmer.

grautur, n., porridge, stirabout;
  muddle.
grös, n., herbs; pasture; Iceland
  moss.
guð, n., God.
guðdómlegur, l., divine.
gæska, n., goodness, kindness.
gæsla, n., watch, keeping.

H.

heilvita, l., sane.
heimfýsi, n., longing for home.
heimleiðis, atv., homewards.
heimsálfa, n., quarter of the
  world.
héla, n., hoarfrost, rime. S.,
  be covered with hoarfrost.
himingeimur, n., expanse of heaven; space.

hjartkær, l., beloved.
hokinn, l., bowed, bent.
hokra, s., keep a small farm.
hragla, s., drizzle.
hraglandi, n., drizzling shower.
húm, n., dusk, twilight.
húma, s., grow dusk.
hvirfilvindur, n., whirlwind.
hvítna, s., become white.

I.

ilmur, n., sweet smell, fragrance.
ís, n., ice.
ísa, n., haddock.

ísaumur, n., embroidery.
ísing, n., freezing rain.
ísjaki, n., piece of ice.

J.

jarðeigandi, n., landowner.
jarðepli, n., potato.
jarðnæðislaus, l., having no farm
  to tenant; homeless.

jöfnuður, n., equal share fair-
  ness, equity, justice.
jökull, n., ice; icehill, glacier.
jörð, n., earth, ground; soil;
  farm, estate.

K.

kafald, n., fall of snow.
kafrjóður, l., crimson red.
kafþykkur, l., very thick.
kappi, n., hero, champion, cap.
kappkosta, s., strive.
konungsdóttir, n., princess.

konungsríki, n., kingdom.
kyn, n., kin, family, kindred,;
  extraction; race, breed; kind;
  sex; tribe.
kynja, s., wonder.
kökkur, n., sod, lump.

L.

lág, n., hollow.
lagaboð, n., law, ordinance.
landsdrottinn, n., landlord.
landset, n., tenant.
landsgæði, n., flt., goodness of land.
landhlutur, n., landshare.
landslag, n., situation; scenery, landscape.
landsmenn, n., flt., people of the land.
landtjald, n., tent.

lifrauður, l., dark red.
lífsandi, n., breath of life.
lífsbjörg, n., sustenance.
litföróttur, l., strawberry coloured.
ljómi, n., radiance, beam.
lýsa, s., light, illuminate; shine. Announce, proclaim, publish; shew; describe; explain.
lækjarfarvegur, n., bed of a brook.
lækjarspræna, n., little brook.

M.

mannkostir, n., flt., virtues.
menntun, n., education, culture.
mý, n., midge, gnat.
mýfluga, n., gnat.

mývargur, n., plague of midges.
mykja, n., dung, cowdung.
mýri, n., bog, moor, swamp.
myrkur, n., darkness, eclipse.

N.

nístingskuldi, n., piercing cold.
norðurljós, n., northern lights, aurora borealis.

nýabrum, n., love of novelty.
næpa, n., turnip.

O.

óbyggð, n., desert, wilderness.
óbyggilegur, l., uninhabitable.

ofsaveður, n., violent gale.
orrustuvöllur, n., battlefield.

P.

pranga, s., hawk.
prangari, n., hawker.

prentari, n., printer.
purpuri, n., purple.

R.

rjúpkarri, n., cock ptarmigan.
rostungur, n., walrus.
rödd, n., voice.
rögg, n., energy.

rök, n., flt., reason, argument.
rökkur, n., twilight.
rökkva. s., grow dark.

S.

saga, n., tale, story, legend, history. S., saw, cut with a saw.
sameining, n., union.
samhentur, l., working well together, harmonious.
samhljóðan, n., harmony.
skuggi, n., shadow.
skuggsjá, n., lookingglass, mirror.
sparð, n., sheep's dropping.

spói, n., curlew.
spranga, s., walk briskly.
steypiregn, n., pouring rain.
stirndur, l., starry.
stjarna, n., star.
stjörnufræðingur, n., astronomer.
stjörnuhrap, n., shooting star.
stýra, s., steer; rule, govern; direct, manage.
styri, n., rudder, helm.

T.

teista, n., black guillemot, Greenland dove.
tjalda, s., pitch a tent; put up hangings.

tryggð, n., good faith, trustiness; faithfulness, fidelity.
tröllskessa, n., giantess.
tæla, s., seduce; entice, allure.

U.

Úa, s., swarm.
úði, n., drizzling rain.
umsátur, n., siege; ambush.
umboðsmaður, n., agent,
  steward.

upphaf, n., beginning; origin.
upphafsmaður, n., originator.
upphlutur, n., bodice.

V.

Vað, n., ford, crossing.
vaðall, n., wading; shallow
  water; slush. Gabble.

víðatta, n., great extent,
  vastness.
vök, n., hole in ice.

Y.

Ybbast, s., turn angry.
yfirgangur, n., aggression; over-
  bearing, tyranny.
yfirbuga, s., overcome.

yngjast, s., grow young.
yngismaður, n., young man.
yngismær, n., young maiden.

Þ.

Þá, atv., then, there upon.
þak, n., roof, thatch.

þeli, n., frost (in the ground);
  catarrh.
þol, n., endurance.

Æ.

Æ, uhr., ah.
æa, s., say ah! cry with pain.

æðikolla, n., eiderduck.
ættfróður, l., well versed in pedigrees.

Ö.

örn, n., eagle.

öræfi, n., wilderness, waste.

SKAMMSTAFANIR

atv. = atviksorð.
flt. = fleirtala.
fn. = fornafn.
fs. = forsetning.
gr. = greinir.
l. = lýsingarorð.
n. = nafnorð.
s. = sögn.
t. = tenging.
uhr. = upphrópun.

Hidden Observatories

John Bevis

'As the Greeks of old entered Troy in a wooden horse, it occurred to me one day that by the employment of a similar stealthy means I might perhaps enter some of the secrets of the bird world...

'The skin of the bullock is stretched over a wooden framework, rendering it strong enough to carry the weight of a man, and at the same time sufficiently light to be easily deported on the shoulder... Admission to the interior is gained through a long horizontal slit in the skin of the underparts, and the camera, minus the legs of the tripod, fixed upon a little platform in the brisket. The lens peeps out of a hole in the skin of the breast, and through another and smaller aperture above it the photographer watches his field of focus.'

Richard Kearton

The telling photograph of bird life 'at home', undisturbed in its natural habitat, is the one whose subject is oblivious of the photographer. In the 1890s Richard Kearton experimented with field hides, beginning with imitations of archetypal local objects: rock, tree, sheep, etc. In human terms they were a faultless means of disguising a photographer and his equipment, many a passing shepherd – but not his dog – mistaking them for real. Birds too were fooled by the 'lifelike solemnity' of these prototypes, and happily carried on their routines and rituals nearby.

But birds were still considered to have a kind of diminished human intelligence, and further experiment and study were needed to demonstrate that imitative objects make an unnecessarily elaborate hiding place. Add to this that they were cumbersome, expensive and specific in location, and there is no wonder that naturalists started to find simpler alternatives. Even so, these early hides were more than quaint absurdities: they enabled some pioneering intimate studies of nesting birds, and as late as 1938 Cherry Kearton 'did not think that they have ever been improved upon' for diminishing the risk of alarming their subjects.

Stuffed Sheep, Westmoreland Fells
Artificial Rock, Westmoreland Fells

The artificial rocks and trees, with their bamboo, chicken wire, canvas, string, paint and glued-on vegetation, lived on as pantomine props, while in the field more homogenous hides were being erected. Some habitats allowed hides to be constructed, like little model Arts and Crafts houses, of 'entirely local materials'. Here there was no attempt to emulate existing manifestations: it didn't matter what they looked like, so long as they guaranteed the disappearance of the photographer. (In fact this 'disappearance' could be disconcerting, and the naturalist often employed an assistant to accompany him to the hide, 'tuck him in', and ostentatiously walk away. Birds could register human prescence acutely, but couldn't count).

The stone and sod houses were of course cheap and easily constructed in situ. Whereas the artificial rock, to avoid an abrupt intrusion, used to be moved gradually towards the nest over a period of days, the stone house, being immobile, would have been constructed a few layers at a time.

This type of hide, suggestive curiously of the earliest human incursions in the landscape, is still reckoned to be the best of its kind in the appropriate situation.

The most practical modern hide for the itinerant naturalist is the small erect tent, resembling a camping toilet. Its arrayment should depend as much, if not more, on subject than on habitat. Most bird species will take little notice of such a hide, especially after a gradual introduction. Some species, for instance the reed warbler, will ignore even the most obvious hide, whereas others, like the garden warbler, are very easily disturbed. Contrarily, some lapwings behave like reed warblers, others like garden warblers.

Camouflage, we have learned, is not essential, but helps when done well. In flat, coverless country it serves little if any purpose, but where there is an abundance of natural material, and the subject is shy, it is bound to assist. The bulk of the hide may be reduced by digging it into soft ground.

For the rest, it is the silence, patience and resilience of the photographer which guarantees the invisibility of his hideaway.

Uncamouflaged Ground Hide for Kentish Plover, French Camargue
Camouflaged Ground Hide for Red-Throated Diver

136 **Bernard Lassus**

Pour les promenades dans la nature,

In Praise of Walking

Thomas A. Clark

Early one morning, any morning, we can set out, with the least possible baggage, and discover the world.

It is quite possible to refuse all the coercion, violence, property, triviality, to simply walk away.

That something exists outside ourselves and our preoccupations, so near, so readily available, is our greatest blessing.

Walking is the human way of getting about.

Always, everywhere, people have walked, veining the earth with paths, visible and invisible, symmetrical or meandering.

There are walks on which we tread in the footsteps of others, walks on which we strike out entirely for ourselves.

A journey implies a destination, so many miles to be consumed, while a walk is its own measure, complete at every point along the way.

There are things we will never see, unless we walk to them.

Walking is a mobile form of waiting.

What I take with me, what I leave behind, are of less importance than what I discover along the way.

To be completely lost is a good thing on a walk.

The most distant places seem accessible once one is on the road.

Convictions, directions, opinions, are of less importance than sensible shoes.

In the course of a walk we usually find out something about our companion, and this is true even when we travel alone.

When I spend a day talking I feel exhausted, when I spend it walking I am pleasantly tired.

The pace of a walk will determine the number and variety of things to be encountered, from the broad outlines of a mountain range to a tit's nest among the lichen, and the quality of attention that will be brought to bear upon them.

A rock outcrop, a hedge, a fallen tree, anything that turns us out of our way, is an excellent thing on a walk.

Wrong turnings, doubling back, pauses and digressions, all contribute to the dislocation of a persistent self interest.

Everything we meet is equally important or unimportant.

The most lonely places are the most lovely.

Walking is egalitarian and democratic; we do not become experts at walking and one side of the road is as good as another.

Walking is not so much romantic as reasonable.

The line of a walk is articulate in itself, a kind of statement.

We lose the flavour of walking if it becomes too rare or too extraordinary, if it turns into an expedition; rather it should be quite ordinary, unexceptional, just what we do.

Daily walking, in all weathers, in every season, becomes a sort of ground or continuum upon which the least emphatic occurrences are registered clearly.

A stick of ash or blackthorn, through long uses, will adjust itself to the palm.

Of the many ways through a landscape, we can choose, on each occasion, only one, and the project of the walk will be to remain responsive, adequate, to the consequences of the choice we have made, to confirm the chosen way rather than refuse the others.

One continues on a long walk not by an effort of will but through fidelity.

Storm clouds, rain, hail, when we have survived these we seem to have taken on some of the solidity of rocks or trees.

A day, from dawn to dusk, is the natural span of a walk.

A dull walk is not without value.

To walk for hours on a clear night is the largest experience we can have.

For the right understanding of a landscape, information must come to the intelligence from all the senses.

Climbing uphill, the horizon grows wider; descending, the hills gather round.

We can take a walk which is a sampling of different airs: the invigorating air of the heights; the filtered air of a pine forest; the rich air over ploughed earth.

We can walk between two places and in so doing establish a link between them, bring them into a warmth of contact, like introducing two friends.

There are walks on which I lose myself, walks which return me to myself again.

Is there anything that is better than to be out, walking, in the clear air?

Index

Published on the occasion of the Scottish Arts Council touring exhibition of the same name, shown at the following venues:

Maclaurin Art Gallery, Ayr *10 January – 7 February 1987*

Pier Arts Centre, Stromness *7 – 28 March*

Scottish National Gallery of Modern Art, Edinburgh *11 April – 17 May*

Artspace Galleries, Aberdeen *30 May – 24 June*

Collins Gallery, University of Strathclyde, Glasgow *7 July – 8 August*

Crawford Centre for the Arts, University of St. Andrews *21 August – 20 September*